About the author

José Luis Stevens is a psychotherapist, teacher, executive coach and an ordained minister. He was apprenticed for ten years to a Huichol Shaman from Central Mexico and in addition to studying with shamans all over the world, has specific training with the Amazonian Shipibo of Peru. He has studied with Tibetan Lamas, Hindu Gurus, mystics, and a Korean Zen Master.

By the same author

The Power Path: The Shaman's Way to Success in Business and Life

Secrets of Shamanism: Tapping the Spirit Power Within You

Transforming Your Dragons: Turning Fear Patterns Into Personal Power

Tao To Earth: Michael's Guide to Relationships and Growth

Earth To Tao: Michael's Guide to Healing and Spiritual Awakening

The Personality Puzzle: Solving the Mystery of Who You Are

The Michael Handbook

PRAYING WITH POWER

HOW TO USE ANCIENT SHAMANIC
TECHNIQUES TO GAIN MAXIMUM
SPIRITUAL BENEFIT-AND EXTRAORDINARY
RESULTS-THROUGH PRAYER

JOSÉ LUIS STEVENS

WATKINS PUBLISHING
LONDON

This edition published in the UK in 2005 by
Watkins Publishing, Sixth Floor, Castle House, 75-76 Wells Street,
London W1T 3QH

© José Luis Stevens

José Luis Stevens has asserted his right under the Copyright, Designs
and Patents Act, 1988, to be identified as author of this work.

Designed and typeset by Jerry Goldie Graphic Design
Printed and bound in U.S.A.

ISBN 1 84293 127 X

This book is dedicated to all my teachers who taught me something about prayer.

Don Guadalupe Candelario
Don Niko
Herlinda, Enrique and Davide
Mahatma Gandhi
Paramahansa Yogananda
Jesus of Nazareth
Thomas Merton
Teresa of Avila
Buddha
Satnam Khalsa
Babaji
Patanjali
Rumi
Thich Nhat Hanh
Sri Aurobindo
His Holiness the Dalai Lama
Zen Master Seung Sahnime
Lewis Bostwick
Lao Tzu
Black Elk
Chief Seattle
Luk
John Milton
all of Nature
and many others

ACKNOWLEDGEMENTS

In this book I wish to acknowledge my patrons, people who have supported my work with extraordinary patience and goodwill over many years. There are so many more of you and I cannot possibly name all of you here. My heartfelt thanks to you. May you walk through life with everyone you love, showered with ten thousand blessings.

Guy and Janine Saperstein, Jim Reed and Bobbie Shear, Scott and Bibi Carter, Pat Lyles, Michael Flatley, Dennis and Gail Flynn, The Toad Group, The Condor Group, Mark Mueller, Laurie Skreslet, Douglas and Marilyn Soltau, Robin and Liz Puttick, Sigrun Boius, and Brian Arthur.

It is better in prayer
to have a heart without words
than words without a heart.

Mahatma Gandhi

Be the change you want to see
in the world.

Mahatma Gandhi

Prayer for Peace

*T*hank you Spirit for manifesting peace in our world
Thank you for teaching me how to be peaceful
Thank you for the peace I feel inside now
May I be a catalyst for peace in the world
May I live peacefully
I am at peace
I am at peace
I am peace
I am peace
I am peace

CONTENTS

Preface

He was a weathered, dark-skinned older man and we watched him with curiosity as he trudged up the trail towards us leading his gray sugar cane-laden donkey. Although his clothing was little more than faded rags blistered by the bright sun we noticed purpose in his stride and intensity in his expression. Eventually he reached us, two *Norte Americanos* sitting on a grassy slope in the middle of the remote Huichol territory in the Sierra mountains of Mexico. Without hesitation he squatted down on his haunches, looked into our eyes without blinking and asked in excellent Spanish, 'And what has God told you today?'

I was completely taken by surprise and I mumbled something (I don't remember what). How often does a stranger greet you like this anywhere else? He got right to the point. 'I'll tell you what God told me today!' With that he began a most surprising and informative discourse about the state of the planet, what was to come in the future, and what we needed to do about it. He spoke of very difficult world events, extreme challenges for mankind, environmental destruction, climatic and weather changes, war, and economic distress. 'We must all learn to pray and if we do we will receive the help we need to see these times through!' This man was in no way a raving lunatic. He maintained eye contact and spoke with eloquence and authority. I realized we were in the presence of a Huichol holy man and from my studies with shamans I knew that this was not a chance encounter.

My wife Lena and I were on our way to a Huichol fertility ceremony in a nearby village and were awaiting permission to be admitted. Our host, who had just obtained permission for us to participate in the usually forbidden ceremony, came down and interrupted this meaningful exchange motioning to us that it was time to go. Upon being asked about the old Huichol, he laughed and told us that indeed this was one of their respected holy men who was known for his predictions and prophecies. This serendipitous encounter was to have a deep impact on me and has stayed with me for many years. I have not forgotten his admonition to pray regularly and as a result of doing so, I have written this book. And because of our brief meeting he has a hand in it.

FOUNDATIONS

One of my earliest memories is sitting in church between my parents at mass unable to see over the pew in front of me. I could hear the drone of Latin, the occasional bells, and the coughs, sneezes, and shuffling of the congregation. Unable to participate in a more meaningful way, I found myself contemplating my own existence and became totally intrigued by the fact that I was alive and conscious of myself. I had not created myself nor did I remember being created. I contemplated the miracle of being alive here in the present moment, and delighted in the flow of the consecutive moments of now that buoyed me along like a boat on a river of awareness. I became transfixed with the awareness of 'I Am Alive!', 'I Am Alive!', 'I Am Alive!' I felt like the luckiest person on Earth. I don't remember how long this ecstasy lasted, whether it was repeated many times or was a single event. What I do know is that I have spent a great deal of my life attempting to get back to that state of original awe and those early pristine moments of pure prayer. Now in my mid-fifties I am finally getting back to the awareness of 'I Am Alive!', I am Alive!' nothing more. So simple, so true, so freeing.

Until seven years of age, I was fortunate to live in a house in East Hollywood with a mix of palms, eucalyptus and other assorted tall trees, making the place seem like a virtual forest filled with birds in the middle of the busy city. My great love at the time was to climb a particular tree at the front of the house, a tree with many branches, smooth bark and the shiniest green leaves I had ever seen. I would climb up and perch in a favorite cleft between two branches and sit for hours communing with that tree. Just as in church, I had an extraordinary sense of aliveness there, contemplating my own awareness and the consciousness of the tree and the many birds that came to perch and sing there. There I communed daily with my Creator in a state of perfect happiness.

The outdoors was my place to play and contemplate and that I did with great abandon. In these preschool days no one ever taught me to talk to God or Spirit. It just happened naturally as if I had always known what to do. I also spent a great deal of time just listening and I believe Spirit talked to me then, but I now have no recall of what I was told.

Loss of Innocence and Explorations

Although I am from mixed parentage, Protestant and Catholic, I was raised in the Catholic religion and spent many hours participating in mass and ritual, singing in the choir, studying catechism and bible history, and learning prayers. During my school years prayer was rote memorization and something given to me in confession as punishment for committing sins. The fear of sin and hellfire was drummed into me and like most human beings, as I grew older I gradually lost that magic awareness of being alive and created by God. I was not able to recapture the profound awareness of those first few years of my life for many decades. I actively contemplated the priesthood for awhile but this was not the answer for me. I became progressively less aware, more fearful, and more despairing. By the time I reached my late teens I was so alienated that I no longer attended church and gave up prayer altogether. Certainly my exposure to religion as a path to aliveness had not taken me where I needed to go. As I look back now I see that despite setbacks, I was given the foundation of mysticism that I would later use to connect with Spirit in a deeply personal way.

THE ROAD HOME

Since that time I have studied with a number of powerful shaman teachers from various parts of the world, particularly from Mexico and Peru. My wife Lena and I apprenticed for over ten years with Guadalupe Candelario, a wonderful Huichol Maracame (shaman) from the Sierras of Central Mexico. He, an illiterate indigenous man, had a better grasp on Spirit than anyone I have ever met before or since. He had true respect for the creator and lived his life in absolute sync with his values and his understandings of how Spirit works in nature and within people. He taught us that El Dios, his way of speaking about God, would answer all questions and provide a clear path. In order for this to happen in the most effective way, one must talk to God regularly in a deeply private way with an absolutely open heart. This was, I was to find, the key to powerful and accelerated prayer.

When he spoke of God, tears would run freely down his cheeks. He was truly a holy man and he opened up new worlds of awareness for me. He told me that when I had been a child I had been open to God with nothing in the way and then for particular reasons I had been burdened with beliefs that had closed me off. He said I was not shut down from the beginning of my life because Spirit wanted to show me what was possible before life came hurtling in to challenge me. As long as I had that light to steer me, it would always be possible to get back to it and this is exactly the way it has happened. That light has been a beacon that called to me always, and that light is stronger now than ever.

When I was twenty-eight years old and traveling in India, I met a powerful guru who told me that I would one day be a writer and the author of many books. He told me that these books would be of great benefit to the people who read them. At the time I dismissed all this as highly improbable but with time I have come to appreciate what he had to say. Now my intention is that Spirit works through my writing to bring the most benefit to the greatest number of people. Principally it is my intent to be a vehicle for Spirit to help bring people back to their birthright, their relationship with God, their ability to pray to Spirit, to affirm what is positive, and discover their own power, each in their own way. May this book equal that intent.

Introduction

THE SOURCES

You will find much of what I have learned from various teachers about prayers in this book. Some of these teachers are people I have spent many years with, listening and integrating their wisdom. Others came to me in books, teachers whose lives were completed before I was born but who had profound knowledge for me to learn. Perhaps the most important teachings come from my own inner dialogues with Spirit, moments of deep contemplation, and states of heightened awareness, especially in nature.

Almost all of the actual prayers presented in this short book I have downloaded from what I call essence, source or Spirit. Because everyone is connected to Spirit, these prayers belong to everyone. Think of them as free software that anyone can use. They have been given in one form or another to millions of people throughout history. These are reproduced here simply the way they emerged within me in moments of deep contemplation in nature. Alter them, add to them, reformulate them at will to suit your own needs. They are only guidelines and platforms to help you get started or to get ideas for your own powerful prayers.

A few are either age-old prayers or prayers that others have shared in the past. In most cases I have modified these for my own use and share the modified version (updated language) for greater accessibility.

I have deliberately not directed the prayers in this book to any specific personages like Jesus, Allah, the Virgin Mary, Quan Yin, Buddha, Mohammed or Krishna except as illustrations in order to make this book as accessible as possible for the widest variety of people. You certainly may pray to whatever powers you believe in.

For all of these prayers, you may substitute any words you wish for God: Great Spirit, Tao, Allah, Spirit, Brahman, Buddha, Creator, Provider and a great variety of other names all work perfectly well. You will find that I have used the words God, Creator, Spirit, Essence and Provider interchangeably throughout the text. Although some religions have theological definitions for each, here they refer to the same thing: the creator and source of the universe.

What is Prayer?

Prayers are an intensely personal communication with what anyone might consider a higher source of power. For some this power source is a vague notion of something greater than they, for others it is a specific idea or experience of a God or Creator, and for many it is a highly defined deity or saint. Despite what some people think, it is not necessary to believe in any specific deity for prayer to produce results. For the shaman, however, there are certain requirements for prayer to be effective and that is what this book is about.

Prayers are concerned with all the most intense human experiences including entreaties for material benefits, supplications for blessings, requests for opportunities, honoring

Spirit, unburdening grief, releasing guilt, unloading affliction, worshipping, affirming desires, offering gratitude, wishing for escape from pain and suffering, and decreeing how it will be. While most organized religions include specific prayers in their form of worship, religion is not the sole proprietor of prayer. People the world over have always prayed regardless of whether they were religious or not. We know from anthropological studies that prayer is one of humankind's oldest activities and today it is as prevalent as it ever was in human history. People of all races, genders, creeds, and cultures pray in many forms and styles.

Despite all that is written about prayer, many people still do not know that prayer is a science as well as an art. There are ways to pray that are more effective than others and some styles of prayer that are downright destructive, as you shall see.

Bear in mind that for shamans and indigenous peoples prayer is more than words but rather a way of living life. They would be inclined to say that their life is a prayer, from gathering and preparing herbs to cooking, from building a shelter to visiting relatives, all is done in the spirit of prayer. All the world's great spiritual teachers and mystics have stated in one fashion or another that to pray unceasingly brings the greatest results. So there is a kind of universal agreement that prayer is something that can be lived, acted out, and spoken as well. In all truth prayer is a way of being, a perspective, a profoundly personal and sacred orientation to the world.

This book has three aims. The first aim is to present for you the seven developmental levels of prayer. When you understand the evolutionary steps to prayer you are in a position to choose a method that is more powerful and fits your needs better. The second aim of this book is to suggest ways of praying that promote well being and build power the shamans' way. The third aim is to offer a number of effective prayers as platforms for you to build upon with your own creations and additions.

The overall goal of this book is to empower you to become a person who prays regularly for greater advantage to yourself and the world at large. The more people who pray well, the quicker this world will evolve from primitive conflict behavior to life supporting and empowering activities that are our birthright.

Part One:

Powerful Prayer

While we usually think of prayer as a one-way monologue to the creator, powerful prayers always end with listening. As I learned from Don Guadalupe, the listening part creates a dialogue or two-way stream of communication. This is one of the definitions of effective prayer. After listening and dialoguing with Spirit it is then imperative to put whatever was learned into action. That is Spirit in action.

Let us begin with some simple keys to praying for maximum benefit. After all, if we are going to spend some of our lives praying, why not make the most of our time praying to have maximum effectiveness.

THE NINE KEYS TO SUCCESSFUL PRAYER

1. Staying present: When stated in the present, as if the object of your focus were already true, your prayers have greater power.

2. Praying from the heart: Prayers stated with emotional intensity provide the fuel that propels prayers and affirmations into reality.

3. Clear wording: Prayers that are clear, unequivocal, concise, and focused produce the best results.

4. Praying without doubt: When you choose to pray without giving any attention or energy to doubt, you are affirming your trust in Spirit, thereby sending affirmative energy to creating what your soul desires. A prayer or decree can leave no room for doubt.

5. Praying with 'I Am': An effective prayer makes frequent use of the words 'I Am' focusing on the source point in the heart.

6. Praying with inspiration: Prayers that are inspirational, dramatic, and luminous are most powerful. Prayers that entrance us with rhyme, repetition, or rhythm have the deepest influence.

7. Praying with intent and vision: When prayers are accompanied by firm intent and clear vision they magnetize the most powerful results.

8. Listening: Prayers that end with quiet meditation, contemplation, or listening are highly effective. The listening part may result in a two-way conversation.

9. Action: Prayers that are followed by some kind of action or application have the greatest possibility of bringing quick results.

Now that you know the nine keys to successful prayer, let us discuss the attitude that you bring to prayer, for this is immensely important in determining their outcome. Your attitude toward prayer reveals your beliefs about your life and about who you believe God is. Here are the seven possible attitudes you can bring to prayer.

The Seven Levels of Prayer

Why can't people agree more with each other's philosophies when they pray? Why is prayer so controversial? Notice how uncomfortable it is to have someone lead a prayer in a way that contradicts your own values. I find it difficult to follow a leader who prays for deliverance from damnation to eternal fires or for overcoming or destroying enemies because these violate my beliefs.

Many prayers are simply not of the same mold and the differences are profound even though almost all human beings pray regularly in some fashion or another. Prayers are so fundamentally different that historically people have killed one another over the form, style, and content of prayers. Millions of people were burned at the stake because their prayers were not acceptable to the authorities of the time. From a shamanic point of view, although there are many contributing factors to these disputes, political, racial, and cultural, the primary cause of friction over prayer is perception, the way a person sees their world.

There are seven states of perception that lead to different forms of prayers and these are at times antagonistic to each other. These different states of perception account for vastly different beliefs about reality and you will find people in every culture of the world who adhere to one or another of them. The latter ones are usually ascribed to mystics and are more difficult for the average person to understand. At the risk of vastly oversimplifying let us look at the seven states of perception and their corresponding levels of prayer.

THE SEVEN LEVELS OF PRAYER

1. Kill my enemies; make me strong over them

2. Please don't punish me! I've been bad; save me!

3. Make me rich! Give me, give me, give me. You are great as long as you give me.

4. Life is so hard! Help me, give me strength, help my loved ones. You have the power to help. I am so confused! I know you are there but why don't you help me, damn it?

5. Thank you for providing for me. I love you! You are wonderful!

6. Thank you for making me in your image. Allow me to know You more and more. I am your servant. Thy will be done.

7. You and I are one. I am peace. Make it so. I am that. I am who I am.

Now let us examine each one of these approaches in more detail. As we go along you may find yourself identifying with several of them because you can hold different perceptions at the same time. This is because each one of us is made up of a complex of sub-personalities that each clamor for attention and gratification. It is up to you to determine which one suits you best overall.

1. Kill my enemies; make me strong over them

When I was a child in grade school, there were several bullies who regularly made my life miserable by threatening to hurt me. They would taunt me, steal my books, take my bicycle and generally make my life miserable. I prayed to the Saints and to God for help to protect me from them and, I must admit, to make them pay for what they were doing to me. Little did I know that my prayers were primitive, infantile, and would do me more harm than good. I was affirming my helplessness and praying for harm to my enemies.

The first and most primitive form of prayer coincides with a basic survival orientation. 'I want to survive at all costs and I need help from the gods to be strong and smite my enemie's. This kind of prayer is the prayer of war and it is found throughout the Old Testament. Prayer of this sort is self-centered and shamanically speaking has little power to effect change or make a difference. Here everyone thinks that the gods are on their side helping them to slaughter the others. This form of prayer is based on terror, separation, and total distrust of others. People praying in this fashion are usually deeply superstitious, fearful, and can even be dangerous to deal with.

Another variation of this type of prayer would be prayers to Satan and dark forces to overcome enemies.

2. Please don't punish me! I've been bad. Save me!

As a child in school I often believed what my teachers told me, that I was sinful and would go to hell unless I went to confession and said many prayers of restitution. I would beg God to forgive me and ask for mercy over and over again, thinking that if I whined enough I might be spared the everlasting fires of damnation.

The second level of prayer coincides with the perception of a toddler, that of a child to a parent. Please don't punish me for being bad and breaking the rules. Take care of me, save me from badness, evil, and satanic forces or demons that I am helpless to fight off unless you protect me. This style of prayer is usually in the form of pleading, whining, and begging. The person usually refers to the creator as a father or a powerful and angry God who metes out punishment.

3. Make me rich! Give me, give me, give me. You are great as long as you give me what I want.

Throughout my childhood, at Christmas time I would always include prayers to ask God to bring me wonderful toys and presents. Later I would pray to ask God to help me do well in a baseball game or track meet. I even remember asking God to help me get a date with a particular girl. I would promise God all kinds of sacrifices if He would just answer my prayers. I became good at bargaining with God.

The third level of prayer is that of a child about ten years old asking the parents for more toys or cookies. This approach to prayer treats God as a kind of Santa Claus who is supposed to deliver an endless supply of goods and riches. At this level, if one becomes rich then it means God has favored them and they deserve more, even at other people's expense. If one is poor then God has not favored them and no one need help or support them. According to this belief the poor have only themselves to blame for their travails.

At this third level God is a force that will punish those who believe differently. 'We are right and saved, you are wrong and damned' meaning that God is not going to deliver toys to your house but will deliver plenty of them to mine. From a shaman's point of view this form of prayer is still weak because it divides up the world into good and bad people and emphasizes toys as the main focus. A person may succeed in actually acquiring these toys but the toys are impermanent and not ultimately satisfying. Sometimes the toys turn into a big problem, giving rise to the admonition, 'Be careful what you pray for, you might just get it.' This third level of prayer is likewise based on the fear of not having enough.

4. Life is so hard! Help me, give me strength, help my loved ones. You have the power to help. I am so confused! I know You are there but why don't You help me, damn it?
When I was a teenager I would often get so frustrated praying to God without results that I would rail against Him and feel totally martyred that 'He' seemed to help other people but not me. I would list the extra things I did that would make me more deserving but to no avail. God seemed silent and distant, perhaps not there at all. I was reduced to a sniveling whiner who resented God when my prayers remained unanswered.

The fourth level of prayer corresponds to an adolescent theme. Life is hard and complicated and certainly filled with suffering. Even though one has wealth, they may not have peace of mind, serenity, or tranquility. There are so many questions and there is so much stress at this level. Compassion and understanding are awakening but life can be so very confusing at times. Prayer at this level is a mix of pleading one minute, despair and disbelief in another, and angry railing at God at other times. It is as if the person is saying, 'Where are You? I know You are there. Why don't You help me? Why did

You make this world with so much suffering? Why do bad things happen to good people? Why do bad guys seem to have all the luck? Well if You aren't going to help *me*, at least You can help my family and loved ones.'

Again, from a shaman's point of view there is not much power in this form of prayer unless one is truly focusing on an area without internal conflict, such as help for others. There is much distress and fear in this style of prayer and these emotions can rob it of its effectiveness and contribute greatly to limitation and negativity. The results can be downright disagreeable because of the resentment involved.

5. Thank you for providing for me. I love you! You are wonderful!

As I grew older, occasionally I would break through my resentment and feel genuine gratitude for the chances and opportunities coming my way in life just as I had as a small child. My heart opened and I would realize that indeed I had been blessed to be here. I saw that my life was an extraordinary gift of opportunity.

From the shamanic perspective the fifth level of prayer is the beginning of real power and corresponds to the maturity of young adulthood. The fog of confusion and anger begins to clear and it dawns on the person that being alive is an extraordinary gift. The person recognizes that they did not create themselves but they were dreamed up, created, and given the opportunity to be awake, aware, and conscious. This is an extraordinary miracle for which one gives thanks over and over in a state of awe and wonderment. The heart begins to open and love pours out to the great provider and Creator of the whole universe. Instead of the small child begging, manipulating, demanding, and whining, the young adult is sophisticated enough to acknowledge the gifts that have already been given. There is now not such a gulf between the one praying and the one prayed to.

6. Thank you for making me in your image. Allow me to know You more and more. I am your servant. Thy will be done

Only recently in my life have I become reacquainted with the powerful God experiences of my early childhood, the miracle of awareness of being alive and conscious moment by moment. Spirit has shown me that in my heart I can find the source point for the life force and the doorway to all potential and all creation.

To a shaman, the sixth level of prayer is truly powerful. This level is associated with real maturity, the perception of an older adult who is a veteran of much life experience. This level is also characterized by gratitude and a recognition that the source of the life force is inside the heart. The Creator is distributed into every particle of the body and is the life force that provides consciousness and awareness to everyone. God is not out there but in here and therefore there is no separation from the Creator and provider of everything. Now, an eagerness to know God more and more begins to take over and there is an acceleration of awareness of the presence of God everywhere. Prayer is about acknowledging the connection, the communication within, the actualization of the energy of source into everyday living. For the shaman prayer is about decreeing how it is.

At this level the person realizes that they are supplied by God moment by moment; that God is dreaming them up thousands of times a second and that they are truly made of God stuff. They are God's eyes and ears, a reflection of source, a projection of a tiny part of God into the physical world, there to explore and create in God's name.

Prayers at this level reinforce the connection and recognize the huge responsibility of being powered by God to be a mini creator, doing as God does by creating reality moment by moment. Here prayers assert that there is only God's will and that it can all be taken away in an instant if that is what Spirit wishes. Prayers announce 'Thy will be done' knowing that to resist Spirit is utterly futile and to recognize that there is only Spirit working through everything, allowing us to enjoy the universe that Spirit has created.

At this sixth level, prayers turn to decrees: 'Spirit, through you I am healed.' 'Spirit, expand and sustain my success and happiness.' 'Spirit, may all beings be illuminated with the light of peace.' This is the realm of the shaman.

7. You and I are one. I am peace. Make it so. I am that. I am who I am.

Level seven prayers are difficult to speak about because they go beyond words. They are a powerful recognition that occurs during meditation and contemplation on the nature of reality. These prayers are more like experiences than verbal statements. Nevertheless this type of prayer asserts that Creator and self are one. There is no other, no separation, no duality, only integration and wholeness. The person who prays in this fashion asserts that 'God' is a state of being and that all suffering is a product of the illusions of dreams that people make in their ignorance of Spirit. When this ignorance is banished in the light of consciousness, the individual recognizes that there never was a problem, never was separation, truly never was banishment from the Garden of Eden, so to speak. God is; I am; I am that; That is God; May it be so.

This level of prayer is for advanced practitioners and corresponds with the maturity one might find in an elder who has become a master late in life. Nevertheless it is an approach well worth striving for no matter what your age because the benefits and the results are so profound.

MIXING LEVELS

Now bear in mind that if you are praying at level one you will not be able to understand anyone praying at any level ahead of you. You can only understand the prayers of those levels you have already passed through. If you are finding some of this difficult to understand, where it becomes cloudy is your edge where you are growing. A person who, for example, is praying at level five can understand the points of view of all the levels prior, but not ahead of them. This phenomenon is responsible for grave misunderstandings about how to pray the world over. For example you might regard the prayers of level six as sacrilege or heretical if you are at level two or three.

This is also the reason why people praying at the more advanced levels sometimes regress in a moment of stress to more primitive forms of prayer. Under extreme conditions an adult might regress to the adolescence or child level before coming to their senses.

PRAYING EFFECTIVELY

In this short book you will find prayers that fit levels five, six, and possibly level seven. These are the levels where prayer has the greatest power to make a difference. When you acknowledge the power of being connected at the deepest levels, you gain access to the greatest powers of the universe. As a helpless victim you plead and whine but this only affirms and reinforces helplessness and victimization. As a child asking for presents you can only hope that you have been good and that an outside force will bring them. As an angry, confused, and suffering being, you can only hope for some relief, again from an outside force.

The minute gratitude appears you are on the shaman's track of power. On the one hand the Creator requires no thanks, no worship, no acknowledgement. Think about it. A perfect being makes no demands. Yet gratitude is a powerful step on the path to recognition because it opens the heart to God, and that reduces the sense of separation.

The more you assert your connection with the Creator, the more powerful you become. Eventually when you can see no more separation between self and Creator, all power becomes available. This is not sacrilege or heresy; it is the truth that all the great saints have discovered.

THE POWERFUL AND ESSENTIAL 'I AM' DECREE

Not until I remembered the importance of the words 'I Am Alive' from my earliest childhood did my prayers become truly powerful. Because of my many years studying eastern philosophy I was under the impression that to say 'I' was filled with ego or self importance and should be avoided. Little did I know that because of this my prayers were missing the mark, and missing the key to opening the heart. Once I saw that 'I' does not refer to ego or false personality but to essence, I understood its value. 'I' is a shared 'I' referring to everyone's 'I Am' state.

'I Am' are two of the most powerful words anyone may ever utter. These are the formative words of creation and they are what align us with Spirit better than almost anything else we can say or do. Just thinking the words 'I Am' invokes the universal life force given to us by Spirit, that energy that keeps us alive moment by moment. A singer reported to me that before every major performance, when he experienced terrible stage fright, he would repeat to himself over and over the words 'I am' and gradually he would calm down completely. When he went on stage he then sang from his soul and his performances were magical.

'I Am' is utterly personal and refers to our total uniqueness as beings. It applies to individualized consciousness, the platform from which we each co-create with Spirit. Paradoxically the words I Am is universal referring to the I Am in everything. Throughout this text the words 'I Am' are synonymous with the word 'essence'. Each human being has an essence that is the sum total of who they have been, who they are now in this moment, and how they present themselves to the world. This essence, sometimes called soul, is the source of each person's life. Essence is created by Spirit and is each person's link to the Creator.

All vowel sounds are significant mantras, special sounds that open up specific areas of awareness. In the words 'I Am' there are two vowel sounds. Notice that the A sound is related

17

to other important spiritual words such as Amen, Allah, Yahweh, and Aum. The sound of the word 'Am' opens doors or energetic pathways to the infinite. You will have to experience this to understand it.

In his most powerful teachings, the great shaman Jesus, who always taught by example, used the words *I Am* with great deliberation. '*I Am* that *I Am*'; '*I Am* the resurrection and the light'; and '*I Am* the light of the world'. Jesus, like so many great spiritual teachers referred to meditation and prayer as the way to redemption. 'If your eye be single your body will be filled with light'. Here he refers to the process of turning the eyes upward and inward and focusing deeply within. It is not by accident that 'I' the English vowel, is also the same sound as the word 'eye', the doorway to the soul. They each evoke the same thing, light. The single eye in the forehead sometimes called the third eye is the 'Eye' that sees 'I', not ego, but Spirit.

When praying, use the words *I Am* frequently but never to refer to something negative, only to positive aspects. Throughout the text I have italicized the words '*I Am*' to remind you of their power. When you come across them it is a good idea to feel these words deep in your heart.

Notice that when referring to anything difficult *I Am* is never used. Negatives are referred to in the past as if they are gone already.

People praying in a group may use *I Am* and still be connected as a group because ultimately 'I' refers to 'Us' or 'We'. 'I' is more true however, because there is only one behind the many.

COMPLETING THE CIRCUIT

Many years of my life passed before I discovered the ultimate key to prayer. Like so many truths the key was right in front of me all along, but even though I saw it, I didn't really grasp it or understand it. With clues and hints coming from my shaman teachers and from my own praying, I finally awakened one day to what that key was in a great 'Aha' experience.

The magical key to effective prayer is completing the circuit with Spirit. Inside the human heart is a tiny port where essence is plugged in just like the connection between your computer and the wall socket. Essence or Spirit animates much of the physical body from that tiny little spot inside the heart, no bigger than the size of an atom. This is where the juice for our aliveness and awareness provides life to the body. This source for our lives is consistently buzzing twenty-four hours a day from the moment of our birth to the moment of our death right there in that tiny port.

I discovered that when I put my attention in that spot I always feel good. This is why I call it the 'Glad to be alive spot'. To get a rough sense of where it is, find the sensitive spot in the center of your sternum and press there lightly. The source spot is just behind and to the left in the top right side of your heart, the location of the sino atrial node. Physiologically this structure is responsible for creating the electrical impulses that is the source for the beating of a healthy heart. Here Spirit pours a constant stream of intelligence and life force into us as a pure blessing and gift of light.

According to shamanic tradition, the life force that comes streaming into the body from deep within, a non-physical dimension of spirit, first enters the medulla oblongata in the brain stem. From there it is distributed both upwards and downwards through the central nervous system to two specific ports. One branch is directed into that tiny port, the sino atrial node in the heart. The other branch is directed upwards into the pineal gland in the central top part of the head. The Native American Hopis from the south-western United States call that port in the top of the head 'Kopavi', meaning 'the open door'. From the medulla the life-stream penetrates into the pineal gland in an intense arc of brilliant pure light. The stream of life force then flows to other key areas of the body where it is further distributed throughout the nerve tree to all the atoms, molecules and cells that make up the body. This is referred to as the tree of life by shamans and mystics. From the mystic point of view the entire body is composed of pure light from Spirit so light plays an important role in the wording of shamanic prayers.

That life force coming in through the medulla oblongata is often eventually dispersed and used up with the activities of everyday thinking, feeling and acting. I discovered that praying under these conditions of leakage doesn't get very far because the circuit has not been completed. The secret to successful prayer is to complete the circuit by returning the life force back to the sacred source spot in the heart, specifically by focusing intent there and using the mantra 'I Am'. This opens the door to the heart. It has been said over and over again by great spiritual teachers that the entrance to heaven is through an open heart. Shamans and mystics the world over say that to enter the spirit world where the source of all things lies, one must have an open heart. This is why they use drums during ceremony and prayer because drums mimic the heartbeat. So directing awareness, gratitude and love back to the essence plug-in spot in the heart completes the circuit. Only then will prayers and decrees have their full dynamic power.

To pray effectively one should always direct attention to this source atom in the heart first while reciting '*I Am*' to engage it. Once you feel the buzz of life there, you are ready to pray. From a shaman's point of view prayers offer directions to what you want Spirit to do. They are like decrees such as 'Spirit, thanks to you *I am* enjoying perfect health and happiness!' And, 'Spirit, I am thankful that *I am* filled with your love and prosperity!' Or 'Spirit, take charge of my thoughts and feelings, erase all negativity and doubt. Guide me to manifest myself as healthy, wealthy, and wise'.

GOOD POSITIONS FOR PRAYING

According to shamans everywhere certain postures and positions are prayers without words. For example an ancient Toltec position of prayer is the following: The shaman stands facing the sun with legs apart and knees bent; the back, shoulders, and head are arched far back; the face is straight up toward the sky and the arms are outstretched to either side, horizontal with the shoulders; hands palm upward and fingers outstretched. The posture is a prayer of complete surrender to Spirit. The heart is completely vulnerable and is given symbolically as an offering to Spirit focused toward the sun. Eventually this posture spread northward from Mexico and was adopted by the Lakota Sioux as part of their Sacred Sundance ceremony.

There are a great many such postures each with their own meaning but a detailed explanation of these is beyond the scope of this book. Here I will focus on simple and obvious postures that you may adopt for your powerful shamanic prayers.

You have a variety of choices regarding posture and position while praying. You can truly pray anywhere, in your car, in the elevator, in the bathroom, on an airplane, or walking on a crowded urban street. Ultimately there is no right place or right way but here are some tried and true suggestions for best results.

I spent many years of my childhood on my knees praying on a hard wooden floor or on a kneeler in church. Perhaps this is why I do not prefer kneeling while praying any more, especially since I had surgery on my right knee. You, on the other hand, may find it your best position so do what comes naturally. I have never seen a shaman pray on their knees and therefore the positions I mention here include everything but kneeling.

STANDING

This form is inspired by the ancient Taoist tradition whose foundation in the distant past was shamanism. Great Taoists like Lao Tzu are some of the world's most knowledgeable sources about how to pray effectively. You can benefit by following their example.

Stand with your heels together, toes angled 45 degrees apart.

Keep your knees bent so that if you look down you no longer see the tips of your toes.

Hold your spine erect with your tailbone tucked in to elongate your spine.

Hold your head level and balance your weight equally on both feet, preferably just behind the balls of your feet at the bubbling springs point.

Relax your shoulders.

Hold your arms down but slightly out to the sides as if a tennis ball were in your armpit, elbows slightly bent, palms facing forward as if you were absorbing the environment in front of you.

Or hold your arms out in front with arms curved around, palms facing in as if you were holding a large Buddha belly.

Place the tip of your tongue on your palate just behind your front teeth.

Keep your eyes lowered or focus them at the point between your eyebrows. These produce different results. Experiment and find what suits you best.

I have found praying in this fashion to be very effective. It allows a nice energy flow without any cramps or blockages. Everything is open and psychologically this is very important. It is actually a state between total rest and absolute readiness. In addition it induces a slightly altered state that is highly beneficial to shamanic prayer. A final step would be to raise your eyes to the point between your brows.

SITTING

If you can sit easily in the lotus or half-lotus position then you may find this effective (Japanese Zen Buddhist method). Being a westerner, I cannot sit this way for long, especially as my knee cramps up since I tore the cartilage.

Otherwise sit in a chair with arms resting lightly on your thighs, palms facing up receptively (Western method).

You may choose to place your palms together in the prayer position over your heart (Christian prayer and Hindu mudra position). A mudra is a specific set of hand positions that have a powerful effect on one's state of mind.

Or you may rest your hands just below the navel, right hand resting in the bowl of your left hand, tips of the thumbs lightly touching (Tibetan Buddhist or Zen mudra).

If you know your mudras you can choose from various Tibetan or Hindu mudras. You can read up on them in other books. These can be powerfully effective but to explain them here is not the main focus.

Keep your feet flat upon the floor.

Keep your head level with your eyes slightly open to keep from falling asleep or focus on the point between your eyebrows.

LYING DOWN

Lying in bed is not the best place to pray because of the tendency to go right to sleep, unless you pray upon awakening or are confined to a bed.

Lying face down on the ground

Lying on the ground spread-eagle facing down is a great way to pray. You may lie with your head on its side facing either way. This is the suggested position for indigenous shamans and mystics for being in touch with the Earth. Although it may sound strange, praying to Spirit in this position can be an intensely moving experience. When your heart is beating next to the Earth you are connected in a way that is unequaled. I once cried for two whole hours on a beach in Baja, California in this position. I gave the Earth all my sorrow and finished up nice and clean.

Many people think of heaven and God as upward and hell and damnation as downward, making this position seem a little odd at first. With a little experimentation you will find that it is powerful to consider the creator as the foundation underneath us as well as the heavens above.

Face up

You may also wish to lie outdoors on the ground face up, with your back to the earth. Imagine your body is a seed in your abdomen. Then free your mind and let it soar as far upward as it wants to go. Pray with an open heart.

WALKING AND RUNNING

Walking is an excellent way to pray. Simply choose a quiet path and walk very slowly concentrating on your prayer.

Many people spend hours every day running. This is also an excellent time and way to pray. I used to run seven miles a day and found this to be a wonderful time to commune with Spirit.

Whether you are walking or running, an excellent concentration is the following. Imagine that your essence within you is standing still at the center of the universe no matter how fast your body is going. You imagine that your body is moving forward and your eyes are sensing an ever-changing landscape as if you were in some sort of virtual reality experience. Essence is always at home not going anywhere. The physical body has the experience of moving about in a physical environment. Are you moving or standing still? This depends on what you are identified with. Try identifying with Essence and you will have an interesting and profound experience.

GOING DEEPER

Even when you are walking or running your essence is absolutely still in one place. Now get the idea that your personality is busy fabricating an ever-changing environment, mapping it and creating the whole world moving around you. Get the notion that all the trees and plants, people and animals in your environment are projections from Spirit into a three dimensional fabricated physical environment made to look like the recognizable world. The world looks like it does because all these creatures are fabricating it, each from their point of view. Each creature's essence is not moving and each one is at the absolute center of the universe. The illusion is that they are in different places.

They are all versions of God experiencing God-self.

Mentally say hello to each as you pass them on your fabricated adventure. This is closer to reality than most people would ever want to admit. People used to think the world was flat. Now we laugh at that notion and say it is round. Some day we will laugh at that notion and say it is a construct and only appears round to our eyes and brain. Perhaps there will be further developments beyond that.

This entire exercise is a great way to prepare yourself for powerful shamanic prayer.

GESTURING

Most people are taught to sit very still with head bowed and hands folded while praying but using gestures, or what shamans call magical passes, can be tremendously beneficial and will produce results faster. If you watch various types of priests officiating at ceremonies you will see that the more effective ones use gestures freely while praying in front of their group. Don Guadalupe, our Huichol Shaman teacher, would gesture freely and often when praying to Spirit. He spoke out loud from his heart, face to the sky, feathers in his hands spread out, completely expressive in his prayers. Never once did I see him on his knees praying. His prayer was active, mobile, energetic, and life affirming. He saw no reason to abase himself before his creator. He knew God wanted him to stand up straight and tall like a tree or a flower reaching for the sun. In his tradition, this is the greatest sign of respect.

When affirming blessings from Spirit why not reach up to the sky and guide blessings down onto your head with your hands like a Taoist doing chi gong? When affirming being healed why not guide healing with your hands to the place on your body that needs it the most? When honoring Spirit for being everywhere and creating everything why not spread your arms and hands out wide indicating the whole universe? When showering Spirit with love and gratitude why not evoke and spread these feelings outward from your heart with your hands and arms? When affirming 'I Am' why not gesture toward your heart or even touch your sternum with your fingers? There are so many ways that your body can speak naturally along with your prayers, enhancing the words many times over. It may be that at times you are so moved by your prayers that all you can do is gesture, words failing, tears in your eyes. Gesturing in these ways adds immeasurable power to your prayers.

WHERE TO PRAY

There is no right place to pray. You can pray anywhere and everywhere. Yet there are particular places that are known to make prayer more powerful and luminous. I recommend praying outdoors with nature whenever possible: on a beach, under a tree, in the desert, on a mountaintop, or rock outcropping. These are the places Jesus, the Buddha, Rumi, Krishna, Saint Francis of Assisi and other great saints chose to pray. Why not follow their lead? I spent many years of my later childhood praying in church. While there is a certain power in people praying together in a traditional place of worship, I now prefer the outdoors as my temple just as I did when I was a small child. I feel better there. You should choose your preferred places as well.

There are some special places in the world that have great power and are wonderful places to meditate, contemplate, and pray. I have found the following places extraordinary for inner work:

- The great stone circles including Stonehenge and Avebury; Glastonbury Tor and Abbey; and the great cathedral in Salisbury, England.

- The great cathedrals – the Pyrenees and the Alps in Europe.

- The Redwoods; the Giant Sequoia groves; Yosemite; the Sierras; the Big Sur Coast; Death Valley; Mt Tamalpais; Mt Lassen; and Mt Shasta in California

- Chaco Canyon, Ghost Ranch, The Sangre De Christo Mountains, Chimayo, and Santa Fe in New Mexico

- The Valley of the Gods; Hovenweep; Arches, Zion; Bryce; Capital Reef; and Canyonlands in Utah

- Canyon de Chelly; Sedona; Wuptaki; the Chiricahuas; and the Grand Canyon in Arizona

- The Grand Tetons in Wyoming

- Mesa Verde; the Great Sand Dunes in Colorado

- The temples in the Yucatan, especially Tulum

- Baja California; Wirrikuta; and the Great Pyramids of the Sun and Moon in Mexico

- The Canadian Rockies and the plains in Alberta, Canada

- The Hawaiian islands

- Machu Picchu; Lake Titicaca; Amantani; Huaylay; the Amazon Jungle; Madre de Dios; the Andes;

Cuzco; the Urubamba Valley; Sacsayhuaman;
Quenko; Puka Pukara; Tombomachay; Pisac;
Ollantaytambo in Peru

- Mount Aconcagua in Argentina

- La Gran Sabana in Venezuela

- The Temples of Luxor; Dendara, Edfu; Kom Ombo;
  Abydos; Saqqara; the Kings Chamber in the
  Pyramid of Cheops in Egypt

- The Himalayas in Nepal and Ladakh

- Varanasi; Rishikesh; Hardwar; and Bodh Gaya in
  India

- Ayers Rock in central Australia

- Thingvellir in Iceland

- Lapland in northern Norway, Sweden, Finland.

These are just some of the thousands of places of power on the
Earth, many of them pilgrimage sites for millions of people. If I
were allowed to go to Mecca, I would probably go there as well.
However, you can also stay right at home, pray in your own
backyard, and be very effective.

Part Two:

Manifesting

PROSPERITY:
WHAT ALMOST EVERYONE WANTS

A lmost everyone wants to be more prosperous no matter what his or her station in life. Some people don't want to admit it out loud but quietly they wish they had more opportunity, more success, more influence, more resources, more talent and so on. There is absolutely nothing wrong with aspiring to greater things. After all, the more resources we have at our disposal, the more good we can do in the world. Having more resources can help you learn what kind of integrity you have. What will you do with the resources when you get them? Hoard them? Abuse them? Waste them? Use them to get richer? Support your spiritual path? Perhaps support and aid others in their endeavors? By having more resources to work with, you will find out more about what kind of person you are.

Sometimes people say to me. 'I know people who have no integrity and they never pray yet they are rich. I know people who are atheists and yet they have money and I know people who pray all the time and they have nothing. Why is that?' I tell them that we do not know what the bigger mystery is that brings about these results. For some people having wealth is a required training course. They need the experience to learn how to use resources. For others it is important that life be challenging and they might have to work harder for what they get, but in the process they learn a lot. The latter has been the case in my life.

The following powerful prosperity prayer is inspired by the great Hindu teacher Paramahansa Yogananda who came to America in the earlier part of the twentieth century and established the Self-Realization Fellowship, a world-wide organization today. He was a great proponent of praying and shared many of his prayers with others. I highly recommend his books on prayer because he is one of the most inspired teachers that I have come across.

He suggested that this prayer be said in order to bring about greater prosperity in every aspect of life. The prayer builds faith, confidence, and self-esteem. This is one of the most powerful prayers I have ever worked with and I have discovered that you cannot say it too many times. There is a building process and the prayer becomes more and more powerful with time. I find it a wonderful practice while on long journeys by car or plane. When I remember to say this prayer, I arrive in great shape.

Ideally, Yogananda suggested saying this prayer nine times in a row: three times out loud; three times at a whisper; and three times as pure thought without moving the lips; to be followed with quiet listening.

I have found it best to say this prayer after chi gong, tai chi or yoga practice, especially in the early morning and/or at night before sleep. It is also excellent and very powerful to do in a group setting. If you are practicing in a group then the designated leader states the words out loud and the group repeats each sentence recited by the leader. Keep to the same cadence and inflection. There are often tears.

 This is my own version of the prayer Yogananda suggested. You may of course adapt it for yourself.

Powerful Prayer for Prosperity

Great Spirit:

You are everything

You are all forms and manifestations

You are infinite creativity

You are all powerful

You are the source of infinite wisdom

You are the source of all beauty

You are all happiness, joy, and bliss

You are cosmic humor and laughter

You have every resource

You are extraordinarily wealthy and rich

You are overflowing with exquisite love

You are filled with the most extraordinary
  energy and vitality

You are total inspiration and compassion

You are all light and illumination

You provide everything

You animate every particle, every atom of the
  universe

You are the source of all life everywhere

And you create me

You are my source

You created me with a supreme act of love
and generosity

You are dreaming me right now

You are pouring life into me

You are within me and all around me

And I *am* part of you

Because you made me and love me

I *am* here cradled in your loving embrace

You made me to enjoy everything you create

You gave me consciousness and self-
awareness

You give me my life

I *am* so grateful to be alive and self aware

I *am* so fortunate and glad to be alive

I *am* so happy to know you are my source
each second

Without you I would not be

You love me and pour blessings upon me
eternally

You animate me and charge me with life

You are my inspiration and illumination

I AM *alive, I Am alive, I Am alive*

And because you are creating me out of
yourself, I *am* rich

I am extraordinarily fortunate

I am a magnet for every resource

I am overflowing with vitality and energy

I am filled with love and good fortune

I am phenomenally wealthy in every way

I have your great wisdom flowing through
me

I am extraordinarily beautiful because I am a
reflection of you

I have the gift of your power available to me
and I choose to use it wisely

I have your stupendous creativity coursing
through me

I am filled with your light and illumination

I am filled with consciousness and life

I am fully awakened and aware

I am fully self-realized

I am extraordinarily blessed

I am remembering

I am becoming

My cells and every particle of my being
dance with celebration because you
made me.

Manifesting Through Prayer

As you have just seen, one of the primary purposes of prayer is to manifest goals, states, and conditions more deliberately and specifically by decree. Often we pray because we desire to transform the way our life looks. We want to change certain conditions like hardship, poverty, or the pain of loss. We would like to draw toward us improved situations like opportunities for success, greater love, and better resources. Why? Because when we are successful we fulfil our birthright as extraordinarily fortunate creations of Spirit. We ask for miracles but it is our very prayers, constructed in a special way, that actually bring these transformations about. Shamans say we are created to be the creators of our lives. Our purpose in being human is to both experience life and to learn to manipulate the primary ingredients of reality, to mold it according to our desires. This is one of the ultimate goals of the shamanic path.

The Four Powerful Sources of Manifesting

There are four important contributors to the art and science of manifesting through shamanic prayer. They are attention, intent, feeling, and envisioning.

Attention

Where you place your attention is what your life becomes about. Attention is critical to creating. Your attention compels life to flow wherever you place it. You cause yourself limitation by giving power to something negative instead of to your own essence and what it is connected to – Spirit. Learning to use the attention correctly requires tremendous discipline but is well worth the effort. Train yourself to bring your attention to what you want and to avoid thinking about what you don't want. In this way you can learn to avoid dwelling on past worries, mishaps, and traumas. This is how you take the energy out of past patterns and it is a prerequisite to erasing personal history, a shamanic technique to increase power.

Your attention depends on your deepest desires. If your desires are positive you will be able to manifest powerfully positive dreams and if your desires are negative then your attention will go there and create your worst fears.

Attention is always present. You attend to the past from the present and you attend to the future from the present. Since the present is the core of your attention, it is best to pray for what you want in the present only. That is, it is better to pray as if what you want is already here. Your prayers are weakened when you use the words 'I hope I will be able…', 'I will someday…', or 'Spirit, if you could see fit to…'.

In order to pray effectively you need to develop the ability and discipline of holding your attention in focus for periods of time. There are literally thousands of methods developed by meditation teachers throughout the ages to accomplish this. You need something you can practice almost anytime, anywhere. One of the simplest methods is to simply attend to your breath. Watch your breath as it goes in. Hold for three seconds and watch as you breathe out. Hold for three seconds and continue. Notice how long you can focus on your breath without having other intruding thoughts. When you have these other thoughts, practice not going off with them. Simply return to your breathing. Notice that you will go off for a while on various thoughts, but when you realize it, don't get upset with yourself. Just return to the exercise. Simple as it sounds it is actually one of the more difficult things to accomplish in life. To discipline the attention is a challenge but absolutely necessary to successful prayer.

Practice five minutes a day and see if you can extend the time you attend to breathing without having intruding thoughts. You may then wish to lengthen the practice. To clear your mind it is a good idea to look at a body of water or the sky and say something like 'clear sky'. Also looking at an icon, picture, or statue is a good way to keep your attention focused. This is not idolatry, simply a focusing device.

INTENT

Intent is what you choose to hold your attention to. Intent is what you are choosing to pray about. Your intent is not mere wishing or hoping but your choice to bring something about, no matter what. For a shaman everything in life is there by intent otherwise it wouldn't be there. Your intent has to do with your certainty that you are creating something new or different in your life. To discover the feeling of certainty all you have to do is review some things you are already certain about. Perhaps you are certain that you love someone. Be aware of how you know that and what it feels like. Now think of other things you are certain of. You are certain that you are alive or you are certain that you have eyes to see with or you are certain that you have shoes on your feet. Take anything you are certain of and become aware of that feeling of absolute positive certainty. Now you must carry this same feeling of certitude over to what you are praying about. That is intent from a shamanic point of view.

The place of clearest intent is in your heart where your

Spirit or essence connection is. By focusing there you will find a constant certainty, confidence, and clarity. Essence is the source of all that is. When you decree from that place you have unshakeable conviction because it is already so at that level. When you have connected with essence at that spot make a clear statement that essence will take over your prayers and keep them powerfully focused.

FEELINGS

Feelings follow from what you put your attention onto. To simplify greatly, feeling is mostly two things. You feel good, you feel bad. Feeling good is related to having your attention on your essence self, the state of being connected, the 'I Am' state. When you feel good all the meridians are open in your body and there is no blockage. Feeling bad is attending to whatever causes discord and separation in your environment and is the product of false personality or ego. When you feel bad there is always a blockage within you similar to being constipated. Feeling bad is an enormous energy leak.

Feelings and thoughts are entwined in a tight embrace. Often feelings drive thoughts and those thoughts can drive further feelings and on and on. The key to creating powerfully is to be able to send your attention to those things that elicit great feelings. Then you will have positive thoughts and further good feelings and it will be easier to hold your attention on these things. Therefore gradual awakening and becoming more conscious is a self-reinforcing endeavor when you put your mind to it because your essence wants you to feel good, already does feel good. With the false personality, the self-important self, it is a different matter and that is where the work is. False personality is the part of you that is constantly getting distracted by drama and phenomena that are external.

No one can become a master creator as long as their feelings run amok. You need to learn to redirect your feelings when they fixate on something inharmonious or negative. Unfortunately, life presents many negative conditions and it is almost impossible to avoid noticing them. A simple glance at a newspaper or watching television news illustrates the point. You cannot entirely avoid the negativity in the world. The trick is not to become a hermit or stick your head in the sand but to learn to observe negativity without getting sucked in and having your day ruined. You must learn to look and say 'Oh, a bombing. People hurting each other. Now where was I? Oh yes, "I Am".' This may sound cold, ruthless, or callous but it is nothing of the sort. You are still having intense feelings but you are choosing which feelings to have. You are choosing to feel the constant intensity of your creative source in your heart while merely marking outside news. To effectively pray, you will find it absolutely necessary to be able to direct your emotion. Otherwise you are at the mercy of one disaster after another and will become powerless and that you cannot afford. Discipline is the only answer. I will speak more about this in the section on overcoming hardships.

Envisioning

From a shaman's point of view we are, each one of us, co-creators with Spirit. The way we create is literally through our dreams. Dreams are a combination of desire, imagination, intent, intensity, and focus. These are also the aspects that propel our dreams into three-dimensional physical reality. Our dreams have lesser or greater power to become actualized depending on the power source we are using. If we are trying to do everything alone, then our power source is like a little battery. It might power a tiny torchlight. However if we are plugged into the great power source of Spirit, then we are harnessing the sun. Interestingly, shamans the world over greet the sun in the morning and say prayers directed toward the sun. They know that the sun is a very powerful form of Spirit and an essential source of power.

Envisioning means to be able to see, sense, and feel what we pray about. Everyone has imagination without exception. The way the imagination works may differ from person to person. You will have to discover your own best way to picture or sense what you pray about. Saying a string of words is useless. Saying words with attention, intent, feeling, and vision is powerful.

Everything in the universe that has form has an energetic pattern like a blueprint. In order to manifest something you desire it helps tremendously to envision the blueprint and then ask Spirit to fill it up with life force. You may ask, 'But how do I know what the blueprint looks like?' If you are having difficulty seeing it in your mind's eye then ask Spirit from the heart to show it to you and wait for it to appear. Then intensely direct the color gold into it and see a green radiance around it. These colors are great for manifesting.

The following prayer uses a Native American format. 'AHo' refers to 'All my relations' witnessing my prayers.

Use this prayer to practice all these components. Say the prayer five times, each time concentrate on practicing attention, intent, feeling, and vision. The fifth time see if you can bring all these components together.

Prayer for Manifesting

I am experiencing peace on earth
AHo-Spirit-Make it so

I am experiencing harmony
AHo-Spirit-Make it so

I am experiencing fulfillment
AHo-Spirit-Make it so

I am experiencing many resources
AHo-Spirit-Make it so

I am experiencing making a contribution
AHo-Spirit-Make it so

I am experiencing loving and being loved
AHo-Spirit-Make it so

I am experiencing vitality and health
AHo-Spirit-Make it so

I am experiencing being a healer
AHo-Spirit-Make it so

I am experiencing being inspired
AHo-Spirit-Make it so

I am experiencing being surrounded by
beauty
AHo Spirit-Make it so

I am experiencing being wise
AHo-Spirit-Make it so

I am experiencing the joy of learning and
growing
AHo-Spirit-Make it so

I am experiencing wakening up from the
dream of separation
AHo-Spirit-Make it so

I am experiencing being fully awake and
conscious
AHo-Spirit-Make it so

I am experiencing being whole
AHo-Spirit-Make it so

I am experiencing being focused on what has
heart and meaning

AHo-Spirit-Make it so

I am experiencing being directed and having
  a clear purpose
AHo-Spirit-make it so

MANIFESTING POWER

In order to manifest we have to generate the power to propel intent into physical reality. Although we are each born with an ample supply of power it tends to leak away wastefully through bad habits, worry, negative thinking and a host of faulty behaviors. Eventually we become depleted and wonder why we have such trouble manifesting anything. All shamans know that to manifest something requires juice and so we need to stop up the leaks and then start gathering and storing more energy.

There are many methods of gathering and storing energy, some physical, some mental, and some emotional. Being out in nature and working with chi gong and tai chi are the most effective ways to gather and store energy physically. Studying how the universe works builds power through mental processes and opening the heart and talking to Spirit builds power through emotion. All three are important to cultivate. Here is a prayer to help you build the power that you will need to manifest your dreams quickly. You can combine this prayer with other methods such as being out in nature and praying at a powerful place. You may also wish to combine it with a chi gong or tai chi practice.

Prayer for Manifesting Power

*G*reat Spirit

You are all powerful

Since you create every particle of this great
  universe

Millions of times each second

There is nothing quite as powerful as you are

I am contemplating your awesome power

I am seeing, experiencing, and knowing it

I am being aware of it all the time

I am learning about power this way

I am asking you to funnel this power

Through the cells of my body

I am experiencing it as light and vitality

I am doing this process often

I am feeling your energy from the planet

Coming up through my feet

I am feeling your power coming up my spine

I am feeling your energy expanding into my chest

I am feeling your power flowing out of my
  arms and hands

I am feeling your vitality flow through my
  throat

And up the base of my skull

I am feeling your power shoot out the back
  top of my head

I am feeling the great vitality of the sky

Flowing down into the forward top of my head

Down my face and throat

Down either side of my spine into the base
of my spine

Mixing and rising again up my spine in a
continuous flow

I am feeling the powerful vitality of your
environment

Your forests, plants, animals, mountains,
deserts, seas

Your sun, moon, stars, wind, and clouds

Your earth, air, fire, and water

Pouring into me through all my pores

Every cell of my body is vibrating with your
great charge

Every atom of my body is glowing with
exquisite light

Every electron is jetting a tiny vibrant blue
flame of life

And this massive collection of flames turning
violet

Forms an immense towering pyre radiating
out though my body

A great charge of your power is collecting in
my reservoirs

Your energy is flowing into my navel and
storing there

Your vitality is flowing into my heart and
    storing there

Your power is flowing into my brow and
    storing there

And each time I follow this practice

I am storing ever more of your great power
    and vitality

This is my birthright

To use as I please

To manifest my dreams

To create happiness and joy

To create peace and prosperity

To alleviate suffering

To bring others to your light as well

Spirit with your support,

I am powerful

I am most powerful

I am enormously powerful

Thank you for making me so powerful

Thank you for providing all these resources
    for free

Thank you for reminding me how to use
    them well

Thank you for your direction

I will use your power wisely to promote your
    great dream

A PERSONALIZED PROSPERITY PRAYER

The following prayer I received from a Sikh woman named Satnam Khalsa who performed deep tissue body work on me a number of years ago. Every time she worked on me she would end with this prayer. I found it so powerful and useful I asked her if I could copy it. I taped it and listen to it frequently to great advantage. I have customized it slightly to meet my own needs. I highly recommend that you tape this yourself so you can listen to it over and over. You can also say this prayer for others. Just introduce their name instead of the word 'me' and change the gender if need be.

Many blessings to you, Satnam, for such a gift.

Prosperity Prayer

*H*ail, Hail, Hail, Honored Great Spirit
Heal me; bless me with health, wealth,
    prosperity, intuition, compassion, light,
    laughter, peace

Honored Great Spirit
Heal me; bless me with health, wealth,
    prosperity, intuition, compassion, light,
    laughter, peace
Honored Great Spirit
Heal me; bless me with health in my mind,
    body, and spirit that I may glow

Bless me with wealth that it may grow

Bless me with prosperity, intuition,
compassion that it may flow

Bless me with light and laughter that it may
show and give me peace that I may know
grace, humility, and serenity

Inspire me with loving, beautiful
environments in my home and in my
work; may these places nurture me,
rejuvenate me, relax me, and energize me
and inspire me with loving, supportive
relationships

Surround me always with people of
consciousness and caliber; people who
will elevate me and support me in my
higher consciousness so that I in turn may
have compassion for others

All blessings, all blessings, all blessings; light,
love, support to me and my loved ones
from the past through my present to my
future

Bless my past that it may be healed; bless my
present that it may be sealed, bless my
future that it may be revealed and bless all
of my prayers known and unknown to me,
spoken and unspoken by me

Fulfill me, bring them to fruition that I may
continue on my powerful destiny; bring in
grace with dignity, divinity, integrity, and
always may I be respected, revered, and
honored.

Part Three:

Knowing Source

WHERE IS SPIRIT?

Even though I spent a great deal of my later childhood in church praying, I had no clue that God really was the source of my experience moment by moment. I thought of God as somewhere higher in the sky, in heaven, a place somewhere else. My God was separate from me and from my everyday experience, mostly disapproving of my attempts to garner a little pleasure and avoid some pain. I believed that God thought of me as a lazy laggard who probably would never make it to heaven. That was a truly negative attitude but at the time I thought it was the necessary stance to take. After all, I didn't want to commit the sin of pride and suffer a worse fate.

Gradually it dawned on me that if God is the source it means that God has to be inside and in between every particle of every electron of every atom in the universe including my own body. That was a true revelation and motivated me to consider other 'scandalous' and 'heretical' thoughts, yet, even this realization didn't make it easier for me to pay attention to source. In no time my thoughts would drift elsewhere and for days I would be completely lost in the dream of everyday life without attending to source one little bit. Nevertheless I was now on the right track. What did it mean that God was everywhere and inside of me as well? Did that mean that God and I were still separate beings? Could it possibly mean that God and I might share the same nature? Oh, blasphemy! Now I was on truly dangerous ground! Imagine the preposterous thought that there might not be so much difference between God's nature and my nature and if that was the case could I really be such a lazy worm of a being? Perhaps if I had these thoughts I would actually be insulting God. Or, could it be possible that an aspect of God was an incompetent laggard? So confusing! Little by little the realization grew. There was no other conclusion to come to. God had to be infinite and if so, I was an expression of God. Slowly the implications of the responsibility of this dawned on me. If indeed I was truly an expression of God then I had a responsibility to God to align myself with God's dream. I should pay attention to my thoughts, feelings, and actions. I realized that I had truly been a lazy laggard but instead of feeling shame and guilt over this I was overcome with laughter. How silly I had been!

The conclusion I came to was this: Spirit doesn't care if you realize you are part of God or not. Yet if you do realize it, God or Spirit is very happy because you are very happy. From the shamanic perspective when you realize what your source is, you become more powerful and effective in the world. The more aware you are of source, the more powerful you become. Jesus, Siddartha Gautama, Krishna, Lao Tzu and other great shamans had a profound realization of this fact. With their realization they became extremely powerful.

MEETING SPIRIT EVERYWHERE

Even though we all know that God is everywhere, we so easily forget. So complete is our forgetting that we engage in behaviors that are completely insane such as war, murder, theft, lying, and mistreating one another. Another form of forgetting is the creation of dogmas stating that God is perfect up there in heaven and we are wicked down here on earth. How can God be up there if God is the creator of everything from the inside out? Does this then mean that God creates the evil of this world?

A hard question, but one we should not shirk from. God creates sentient beings out of love and then gives them the free will to co-create. People have the freedom to create events that are not loving, until they eventually remember who they are. God is responsible for everything that happens in the universe so, yes, God allows foolish illusion to be created. But that does not mean that God gets pleasure out of unloving acts. To the creator, they are just illusions that have no ultimate reality, because they are not in alignment with the truth. This is a very difficult thing to understand so it takes a great deal of contemplation. To us humans these painful events seem real for now, but one day they will be like a bad dream that vanishes in a sea of truth, love, and energy.

Sometimes it is very helpful to remind yourself where Spirit is. We so easily tend to forget and become disconnected for a while and that leads to feelings of powerlessness. Here is a prayer to help remind you of where to find Spirit.

Prayer to Meet Spirit Everywhere

Great Spirit you are everywhere
I feel you deep within my heart
I am inside you and experiencing you
Like a flame of light coursing through me

I meet you in this tree
I see you in this cloud
I feel you in this breeze,
I smell you in the fragrance of this flower

You are everywhere I go
Everywhere I stop to rest
I visit you in sleep and in dreams
I visit with you in friends

I pet you in this fur
I eat you in this fruit
I lie on you in this meadow
I climb on you on this mountain

I walk in you in this forest
You are always with me
And *I am* always your manifestation
Playing, working, studying, resting

I sense you inside me
An expanding light intensifying
Deep within my meditation, I feel you
Deeper into silence you penetrate my heart

You filter through my cells and atomic
    structure
You are golden light sweeping through me
You fuel me and bring brilliance to my
    awareness
You flood me with beauty and vitality

And I become these gifts you give me
For *I am* within you and you are within me
I feel your blessings everywhere
I am truly eternally blessed

PARTNERSHIP WITH SPIRIT

According to shamans and mystics the world over, there is great
power in aligning with something more powerful than yourself.
This is what I was taught by my teacher Don Guadalupe. You
always become more powerful when you associate with the
greatest powers around, so, why not create a partnership with
Spirit because that is the greatest force in the universe? There is
absolutely nothing to lose but misery and everything positive

to gain. Offer your services to Spirit and see what happens. Of course, in all honesty, Spirit will probably test you to see if you are serious. In the face of challenging tests, persevere no matter what.

Prayer for Partnership with Spirit

Great Spirit I *am* your ears for you to hear with

I *am* your eyes for you to see with

I *am* your emotions for you to feel with

I *am* your voice for you to express through

My arms are for you to hold with

My hands are for you to touch with

My feet are for you to walk with

I *am* your vehicle, your tool for expression

Use my mind and brain to think with

Use my experience to know your creation with

I *am* your lens to view your vast creation through

Great Spirit I *am* your partner and you are mine

Together we will create

Together we will show kindness and compassion

Together we will be generous

Together we will love and play and enjoy

When you are with me *I am* whole

When you are working with me *I am* healed

Together let us create a healing presence for
all to benefit

We are partners for good, for love, for joy

And let us together join others in partnership
in your name

Until we have all remembered that we
are one

EXPANDING

Spirit is big, about as big as you can get. By contrast being in a human body feels small, yet there are those who make their lives big anyway. Gandhi was a man of small stature and slight build but he shone a giant light on the world. So has Nelson Mandela, Thich Nhat Hanh, Mother Teresa, the Dalai Lama and many others. This is because they know they are more than their relatively minor physical personalities and they know they are connected to the massiveness of Spirit. They can play on a huge chess board. Yet there is a difference between a Gandhi and a Hitler, an Osama Bin Laden or other present-day tyrant. The Gandhis of the world have real power because they have Spirit working through them. Tyrants play with the trappings of power to make up for their smallness and obvious limitations.

Too often ministers and priests preach that we should be small and humble in the sight of God. They preach against vanity and warn of the sin of pride, threatening dire consequences from a wrathful God. This is of course nonsense. We are here to make a difference and that is hard to do by hiding under a bush. When we align with Spirit we become expansive, influential, inspiring, and regal even though we may still speak with a soft voice. Spirit is majestic and uses a huge brush and canvas to create. That Spirit is within each of us and wants nothing more than to actualize, self-realize, and burn as bright a light as possible, like the sun. To the shaman each of us is a mirror to the sun and the brighter we radiate the more of Spirit we manifest.

A Prayer to Expand with Source

*C*reator and Provider
You are huge
You supply every particle of the universe
Radiating light and energy
Creating, energizing, vitalizing
You stretch in every direction to infinity
You are all time, without any limit
You are the brightest light in the universe
You are the lightless light in the endless void
You do not limit yourself regarding anything
You who are too big to name
You are the awesome sound of a thunderous falls

A thousand miles wide
The massive sound of a trillion voices
Singing in harmony, singing in beauty
Singing with rhythm
You are a billion drums beating a powerful,
    driving cadence
To energize, to enliven, to awaken
You are every instrument multiplied by
    millions
Creating the most amazing sound of
    grandeur
And all these qualities of power shine within
    me
I am huge
I am an endless light that radiates from you
    through me
My heart is a giant pouring forth rainbow
    flames
To engulf the earth, the planets, and outer
    space
My mind is enormous, able to stretch to feel
A part of your infinite light
My throat opens like a canyon to sing
To shout
To speak your powerful truth
I am making a difference on this planet
I am participating in a massive awakening

With all my big brothers and sisters

With my great friends from nature

Together we are enormous and powerful and
 great

Because we are expressing you, Spirit

And yet, I can be tiny too, when it is right

Like a babe cradled in your arms

Trustingly sleeping in your graces

Allowing your enormity to comfort my tiny
 form

Until I awaken once more to hugeness

And the wonderful fortune of being a part

Of something so great

CHOICES

As human beings we have the gift and the curse of free will to
make endless choices. Sometimes our choices bring about great
suffering and sometimes great joy. Often we are unconscious
about the choices we are making. Sometimes our choices
happen by default. By refusing to actively choose, we end up
with less than happy results. That is still a choice so there is no
escape. To become powerful it is best to consciously choose the
state of mind that we wish to live in. Here is a prayer that I
have used to assist me in that process.

Prayer of Choice

Great Spirit
I choose to be awake
I choose to remember who *I am*
I choose to remember you
I choose to love
I choose peace
I choose happiness
I choose bliss
I choose to be generous
I choose to celebrate
I choose power, vitality, and health
I choose to use your resources to benefit the
    world
I choose to be wise
I choose to be beautiful and youthful
I choose to see your beauty in everything
I choose prosperity and success
I choose to align myself with your grand
    dream
I choose to persevere in knowing you
I choose to make you my guiding light
I choose light and radiance
I choose healing and wholeness
I choose clarity and focus

I choose to make the right choice

I choose your way, your path, the path
with heart

BECOMING

We humans are always in the process of evolving, becoming the full potential of the seed within us. Yes we are human beings, but we are also 'humans becoming'. We choose what we will become, but when we choose in alliance with Spirit, we accelerate the process of evolution immensely. There is no hurry in infinity of course, but why not cut out some of the suffering?

Prayer for Becoming

**(based on a prayer inspired by Paramahansa
Yogananda)**

*G*reat Spirit

I did not choose to be created

I did not make myself

You chose to create me to share your
incredible being with me

I can only do the best I can

To live up to the great honor you have
bestowed on me

I am in a learning process and I have made
   mistakes

Yet all I want to do is grow and become my
   full potential

To realize myself and realize you ever more

I am a human being becoming, help me to
   become

I am a human becoming, help me to become

I am a human becoming powerful, help me
   to become

I am a human being remembering

Thank you for helping me remember

I am a human being awakening, waken me
   please

Waken me and assist me to become a fully
   realized human being

And may I reach out my hand to others
   becoming

That together we may become enlightened,
   illumined, and inspired

Prayer for Knowing Source

FROM A VISION

*D*eep within my heart is a bursting
   blossoming rose
Infinitely transforming, growing, transfiguring
Evolving, emblazoning with glowing pink
   light
A form you've given me to see
How you arise in me
How you give me life

Behind my eyes is a blazing flame of vitality
Clarifying, clearing, opening, vivifying
Deeply violet in color and intensely bright
Your brilliant presence inside my head
A shape you've given me to see
How you illuminate me
How you inspire me

All around me is a towering funnel
Surrounding me from under my feet to
   the sky
A barrel of your light enveloping my body
Filled with golden flames
Healing, protecting, and buffering me

From the worries of this world

With you as my source
I need not worry
I have everything I need
I am safe
I am happy
I am opening to you

You are forever with me
Showering me from above with your light
You are behind me
Gently whispering me forward
And you are ahead of me beckoning me
Forever forward, forever blissful,
   forever happy

INTENT

From the shamanic world viewpoint, whatever you see in your life right now is what your essence intended. When you understand that your essence is co-creating your life with Spirit you are suddenly free because you can go about recreating your life consciously. The first step is to accept how it is. The second step is to intend something new. This is not as simple as it sounds because to be successful at intending you must have absolute certainty that it will come to pass. The best thing to do in the meantime is 'fake it until you make it'. Practice having confidence in your intentions.

Prayer for Intent

Spirit, you intended for me to be here and so *I am* here

Spirit, you intended for me to wake up so *I am* waking up

Spirit, you intended for me to become a co-creator so here *I am*

Now I am intending to intend what you intend

I am intending to know you better

I am intending to be here fully present

I am intending to awaken

I am intending to experience you every single moment

I am intending to be powerfully conscious

I am intending to be blessed

I am intending to be a singer and a dancer

I am intending to be free at last

I am intending to be joyful

I am intending to be loving and to be loved

I am intending to make a difference

I am intending to be a participant

I am intending to complete my contribution

I am intending to serve with gladness

I am intending to be rich with resources

I am intending to be wise

I am intending to be perfectly healthy

I am intending to be fully charged with
essence

I am intending to spread peace and light

I am intending to die with a big grin on my
face

Because I lived my life with complete
abandon

And I lived with my heart full and spilling
over

Spirit, my intent is your intent

And whatever I see in my life

Is what we intend together from now on

Part Four:

Life Challenges

Hard Times

Hard times are relative. I used to think I had some very hard times in my life. Like many other people I have had experiences that include being beaten; being left for another; being stolen from; having serious accidents; losing large sums of money; being slandered and judged; being passed over for advancement; being ignored; having sickness and family problems; having lost friends to tragic death; having been many times to the emergency room with my children; having been accused and blamed; having suffered miserably from allergies; having struggled financially; having had lungs collapse; having had bones broken and teeth problems; having had cars wrecked; being whip-lashed; being investigated and fined by the IRS; being drafted; being arrested for trespassing at a concert; having had speeding tickets; and being rejected many times by publishers and conference coordinators. Yet compared to others my difficulties have been almost nothing at all. I have had an extraordinary and wonderful life thus far. I am extremely fortunate. Yet when life gets hard it seems over-whelming and feels like it will last forever. Fortunately there are remedies for hardship.

After working with thousands of people, even very successful people, I have learned that life is hard for almost everyone. It becomes hard because we so easily fall into the trap of experiencing ourselves as separate and alone. This sense of isolation breeds deep fear, mostly fear of abandonment, something that is so painful it can actually cause death in severe cases. We are often mistreated in childhood and throughout life by the thoughtless actions of people who neglect our needs because they are caught up in their own dramas. Because we always do to ourselves what was done to us, we learn to abandon ourselves and then we feel abandoned by Spirit in an old psychological defense mechanism called projection. We blame Spirit for what others and we ourselves have done. People seek therapy, medication, and other methods to heal from this terrible dilemma, but in the end there is only one real solution. The solution is to go to the source of the problem and get reconnected to Spirit. This is not necessarily easy but it is absolutely necessary for redemption and healing. It is the shamanic way of healing.

Finding religion might seem like the same thing as discovering Spirit but it may not be. Religion is fine as a means of social gathering but to place absolute faith in an organized system of beliefs is precarious because dogma and external authority does not come from within. To find religion is a hope that something outside will save us and it so often disappoints. From the shaman's point of view beliefs will never satisfy. The solution is 'to know' and that comes from the heart alone. You must know that source is within you at all times and that this source is so powerful, so immense, so awesome that no name can ever be adequate to encompass it, and no dogma can ever do it justice. The power of essence is so expansive that most of us would be absolutely terrified if confronted with even a tiny fraction of it. And yet confront it we must because it is the only reason we are alive and without it we would all vanish instantly. Every great spiritual teaching states this unequivocally and yet we don't listen and instead we persist in becoming horribly lost. Here is a prayer for coming back from the darkness and dealing with depression.

Prayer for Overcoming Depression and Dealing with Hard Times

*G*reat Spirit
Even though I felt discouraged
I know you are supporting me
I just forgot for awhile that you are my
    source
You want me to be fulfilled
Even though I felt depressed
I know you are inside me
I just forgot my connection with you
Even though I've been so anxious
I know you love me totally
I just fell asleep for awhile
And even though I've had a hard time
    focusing
I know your light is shining within me
I just looked away for a time

Even though I felt so much doubt

About my ability to succeed

I know you gave me an abundance of
    resources

You created me to be just like you

 You are supporting me with an endless
    supply

Even though I felt out of control

I know you direct me behind the scenes

I became overly identified with the human
    movie

Getting lost, losing my way

I found myself all alone

I had the illusion that I was not connected
    with you

But Spirit, you are always here

With me, all around me, inside me

You were never gone

I just stopped paying attention

And I suffered terribly because of it

You created me

And are creating me in this very moment

You made me for the sole purpose of
    knowing you

And learning to manipulate your wonderful
    resources

You are infinitely powerful

And anything you are, *I am*

So now I am back on track

Remembering that you are the only game in
 town

You never leave me

You never forget me

You create me with your intention every
 second

Millions of times a second you pulse me with
 life

You are my source and my supplier

Deep in my heart you are plugged in to me

You are my life

 And there is no satisfaction until I
 remember

I am remembering who *I am*

I am healed and whole

I am connected

I am deeply loved every second

You charge me with light

I am healed and whole

I am the flame of essence

I am truth, love, and power

I am healed and whole

Thank you from the bottom of my heart

CONFESSING

Confession can be a powerful healer when it is done properly. When I was a young boy I was raised as a Catholic and was taught to confess my sins to the parish priest in a little closet at the side of the church. I was terrified of confession because I never thought it was right to confess to a priest who I didn't even know, especially when he wanted to know all the particulars and details of my simple fantasy sex life at the time. I felt shamed and I felt even more ashamed when I reported the same set of sins week after week without any change. The priest was supposed to represent God, but he was acting as a man, a lonely sex-starved man. The principle of confession was important, but the way it was carried out was barbaric and lacked integrity.

Surprisingly I relearned the value of confession from the Huichol Indians in the Sierras of Central and Western Mexico. They regularly confessed their sins publicly to the fire (Tatawari) and to their community during all night ceremonies. Their method was to tie a knot in a string for every thing they felt was out of harmony or imbalanced within their own integrity, *pecados* they called them. After many knots they threw the string into the fire and watched it burn while asking forgiveness with all their neighbors watching as witnesses. At the end of the ceremony the entire village was harmonized and healed. There were tears, hugs, and reestablished relations. Hard feelings were released and forgiveness offered.

From a shaman's perspective one does not need an intermediary to confess one's sins. The root of the word sin means to miss the mark in archery. Why should that be a problem? We all miss the mark many times in life and it is important not to get stuck in these mistakes. To confess is to release and forgive one-self. So confessing to the fire, to a mirror, to a notepad, to another loved one all works wonderfully. This is the shaman's way.

The natural balance to confessing is to forgive, a process that completes and closes the circle. Fundamentally to forgive means to give something back, for-give. When we forgive we give freedom back to whoever is confessing. We give space to create fresh and new. We give expansion and love. That is why to forgive is considered divine. It is!

While asking for forgiveness is healing, it is even more healing to forgive oneself and then reassert the connection to Spirit. Spirit doesn't really care if you miss the mark. Spirit knows humans are going to miss the mark because the Creator made humankind to evolve through learning consequences. This involves mistakes and learning from those mistakes.

An Unburdening Prayer

*G*reat Spirit
Sometimes I worried and felt anxious
Sometimes I thought I would lose everything
Sometimes I got angry, raged at my lot in life
Sometimes I compared myself with others
    and came up short
Sometimes I thought I was lost and became
    afraid
Sometimes I felt out of control and terrified

Sometimes I thought people would ignore
me or hurt my feelings

Sometimes I thought I would fail at
everything

Sometimes I thought I had no value

Sometimes I procrastinated because I was
afraid I couldn't do it

Sometimes I got depressed and felt
discouraged

Sometimes I felt sad and lonely

Sometimes I felt I had lost my way

Sometimes I cried bitter tears of regret

Sometimes I felt ashamed

Sometimes I felt guilty and bad

Sometimes I felt the pain of envy and
jealousy

Sometimes I was afraid I would look like a
fool in front of others

Sometimes I was critical and judged others

Sometimes I slandered and gossiped to feel
better about myself

Sometimes I thought I was a fool, not worth
anything

Sometimes I took foolish chances with my
health and safety

Sometimes I refused to listen and thought I
knew better

Sometimes I was impatient with myself and
with others

Sometimes I made people wrong and myself
right

Sometimes I have been prideful and
sometimes I felt low

Sometimes I whined and carried on like a
victim

Because I forgot you

Because I thought I was separate and alone

Because I fell asleep for a short while

Yet you never blamed me

You never judged me

You never took offense

You make it possible for me to be forgiven

I now forgive myself for everything

Spirit, I forgive myself with you as my
witness

I have no right to judge myself

You never judged me

You never took offense

You make it possible for me to be forgiven

I now forgive myself

I *am* forgiven

I love myself

I love you

I forgive all those who have hurt me

I forgive all those who have forgotten me
I forgive all those who have ignored me
I forgive all those who have judged me
I forgive all those who have taken from me
I forgive all those who have insulted me
I forgive all those who have abandoned me
I forgive all the slights real or imagined
I am letting go of all this cargo
I am releasing everyone
I am free, free, free

ANXIETY AND WORRY

When I was younger I spent too much of my valuable time being anxious and worried. It never helped one tiny bit. Worry and anxiety are truly a terrible waste of time and yet they seem to be a pervasive and fundamental problem for many of us. We are mortal creatures in bodies that can be hurt, maimed, or killed. We have sensitive emotional systems that can be painfully attacked. Since we are sentient creatures with frontal lobes for thinking abstractly, we are capable of projecting into the future unlike other animals. This ability to consider the time factor is both a blessing and a curse. Through it we are able to create goals, plan for the future, learn from our mistakes, and compile knowledge. The disadvantage is that we remember pain and horror from the past and seek to avoid it in the present or future. We can project all manner of fears into the future and raise our stress level enormously. Tell a horse that it might be put to sleep at dawn and it will make no difference to the horse at all and it will go on quietly munching away. Tell a human that they might be executed at dawn and they will most likely have a horrific attack of fear that will cause them no end of anxiety and worry even if it is only a remote possibility.

Our biggest challenge as human beings is our ability to associate thoughts. A fear of public speaking, going for a job interview, or asking someone for a date can turn into a fear of actually being physically hurt or killed. In our complicated lives that are so stressful there are no end of worries that keep us up at night and prevent us from enjoying the moments we have with our families and friends. Pharmaceuticals are one method we have devised to ease the pressure of anxiety attacks but they are temporary salves that are also hard on the organs of the body. Eventually they will kill us if over-used. We all need a great deal of help to quell anxiety and stay present. The ultimate help is spiritual in nature.

When dealing with anxiety you have to commit yourself to easing it. You have some responsibility not to indulge yourself in all your fears. From personal experience I know that reducing anxiety must become a discipline or all the outside help in the world will not result in any benefit. Indulging in anxiety is a huge energy leak that robs you of the possibility of breaking free. To become powerful you must erase it at the source.

Here is a prayer to address fear and worry. Notice that the worry is placed in the past and the calm is placed in the present. Even if you are very anxious, saying the prayer will begin to calm you down. That is what it is designed to do. In order to enhance this prayer's effect, you can employ an ancient shamanic technique. Rub the roof of your mouth with your thumb and this will also produce a calming result. This is what small children naturally do to calm themselves before sleep.

Prayer to Reduce Anxiety and Worry

Great provider, I have sometimes worried
    myself sick
And I have had painful anxiety attacks
I have felt so alone when I became fearful
    like this
I felt so desperate for relief but could not
    calm down
I forgot that I had your help
I forgot that I was connected to you always
I forgot that you were deep in my heart
Instead my thoughts raced and I was in my
    isolated head
Now I am home in my heart
Now I feel warmth there, I had previously
    ignored
Now I feel my breath calmly going in and out
And I know you are inside me and with me
And all I have to do is ask for your help
With your help I am quieting my thoughts

With your help *I am* relaxing my mind

With regular out breaths I allow the panic to
release

The fear of the future is not real

The what ifs, the maybes, are not real

I am right here right now

I am OK

You are with me right now

And what will be will be regardless of what I
think

There is a deeper plan and I don't have to
control my life

I am here with a purpose

I am created by you to realize myself

I have never been alone

I am endlessly supported

And I have a contribution to make

My job is to do my best and not to worry

I am calm now

I am calm now

I am calm now

GRIEF, LETTING GO AND LOSS

Life is a never-ending cycle of change. All is impermanent and everything created will be dissolved back into the void whether we like it or not. This is one of the harder aspects of being human because we become attached to many things, our family, friends, possessions, lifestyles, our bodies, our looks, pets, working conditions, and so on. The one thing that is absolutely certain is that everything is changing and will soon look very different. The more we struggle to hang on to how it is, the more painful the loss when it doesn't remain so. All of us need some help now and then with letting go and un-attaching.

At the heart of loss is the experience of abandonment, one of the toughest experiences any human being can have and everyone, no matter how blessed, has had moments of abandonment. We are abandoned when a friend or a pet dies. A divorce or break up is a kind of abandonment and so is the experience of children leaving home. Losing a job, moving, graduating, getting transferred, going off to war are all experiences that can bring up feelings of abandonment. Abandonment brings up a host of complex feelings and emotions like fear, desperation, anger, and ultimately grief. Here is a prayer to address such loss. Remember to start by focusing on the place on the right side of your heart that is the source for essence, the shamanic cure for feelings of abandonment.

Prayer to Handle Grief and Loss

Great Spirit
You have given me everything
You have given me my life
You have given me all my experiences
You have given me all my friends and people
    that I love
You have given me places to live
Pets to love
Places to work
Things I have grown accustomed to
You gave me love and you gave me affection
You gave them to me for awhile
I wanted them forever
I wanted to believe it would never change
But of course that was simply an illusion
And when they went away, I became angry
I became angry with you for taking them
    away
Then I thought desperately of how I could
    get them back
But they were gone, physically gone
And that was a total fact
And I was left all alone
Never to touch them again
And then I remembered

You never promised that anything would stay
    the same
You never gave them to me forever
That was never the agreement
Even though I didn't like it
It's true
They were only on loan
And what a gift that was
You didn't have to give them to me at all
But you did and I *am* glad
What a blessing I have had
They are all forms that are changing
All with the essence of you
And that you is never lost when your form
    goes away
Because you are in all things and beings
They needed to go
To trade in their forms
So they could transform into something new
And though I'll cry and sob and shed tears
    anew
To release the feelings inside
I send them gladly on their way
To another adventure, to greater things
I am accepting of how it is
And someday I'll follow that path

Because forms change but essence remains
And in that way we have never parted
If I attach to the form it changes
If *I am* attached to you its forever
I'm glad there's change
Although it hurts
Because it's a great adventure
I am accepting of how it is
And whenever you close a window
You open a door to fill the loss
And although life has changed
There is new coming
That I could never have anticipated
That's the way it has always been
That's the way it should be
I am accepting of how it is

ON BEING ANGRY

Anger comes from disappointed expectations. Most of the time
our anger is a loss of energy and is unproductive. In our lives
there are moments of righteous anger that actually help
motivate us to accomplish great outcomes and help us to
survive otherwise fatal experiences. Discriminating between
these positive forms of anger and ones that lead to energy

wastage is an act of great wisdom. On the way to that wisdom we make many mistakes.

For most of us managing anger is one of life's greatest challenges and the world is not getting any easier in this respect. The ancient Chinese had a saying, 'Get angry get sick; Don't get angry, get sick.' Theirs is a brilliant observation and suggests that the only way out is to admit being angry or the consequences are horrific for our own health and for the well-being of our relationships.

Denial that we are angry makes anger worse and builds into resentment that is like a slow poison killing off aliveness. Being truthful about being angry is the first step to clearing it, yet, there is a big difference between expressing anger and admitting it. Expressing anger or acting it out is usually destructive and expands the pain in many directions but admitting anger is constructive because it is simply what is so and an admission of no resistance to it.

Here is a little prayer that has helped me manage anger.

Prayer to Help Reduce Anger

Creator

Sometimes I have felt angry

I felt anger surging though my body and I
    felt uncomfortable

Anger invaded my thoughts making me want
    to get back

To take revenge out, to make someone pay or
    feel the way I did

At times I wasn't able to get away from it

I felt angry because I thought life would be
different

I thought it would turn out a different way

I had one idea and it came out another

I have been so disappointed and irritated

I imagined myself to be the one in charge

The one who could be the judge of right and
wrong

The one who could set things right

But that is not really my job

That is your job and only you know the big
picture

Being angry has made me see myopically

I don't know what is around the bend

I can only act honorably and accept how it is
for now

Perhaps I hated in the other what I don't
want to see in me

Perhaps there is something I have resisted
here

Spirit, I ask you to show me what I need to learn

My anger separated me from knowing you
better

So help me forgive myself for getting angry

Feeling angry doesn't make me bad

I know I can let go of this burden and move on

That is what I intend
That is what I want
That is what is best
I am at peace
And when my anger is justified
When I have seen injustice done
Let me speak of it with truth and clarity
Allow me to release it as quickly as it came
And turn to forgiving as soon as I can
That is what I intend
That is what I want
That is what is so
I am at peace

HABITS AND ADDICTIONS

Creating habits is the way we learn the best. We learn to type by teaching our fingers to habitually go to certain keys. We learn to speak a language by teaching our minds to habitually make specific sounds in a certain order. The same is true for driving a car or operating any machinery. Habits are part of our survival machinery, but when they get out of control they can also harm us or even kill us.

We form habits in order to go beyond them. The habit takes over and frees us to do other things. This is how we drive a car. Habits can be quite difficult to change. That is why it is difficult to behave differently from the ways we are culturally used to.

My shaman teachers explained that the danger of habits is that they make us predictable and that makes us vulnerable. A prairie dog rises out of its hole at a predictable 68°F. All a hawk has to do is wait until the temperature rises to 68°F and it can have lunch. To the degree that each one of us is utterly predictable is the degree by which we can be manipulated and that is why advertising works so well.

Sometimes we form habits that can be quite harmful to us and they get such a grip over us that they become addictions. An addiction usually involves one of the pleasure centers of the body that gives a feeling of temporary relief from the pain we feel inside. When a habit becomes an addiction we have lost control over ourselves and that is dangerous. Addictions lead to self-destruction sooner or later.

According to ancient mystery schools the color violet is a powerful healer of addictions. You can work with this color when you feel the press of addiction upon you. Imagine soaking yourself from top to bottom in violet for a few minutes and especially run the color like a flame through your thoughts to clear them out. Lavender, the flower, is also an effective tool to use to fight addiction. Just rubbing some lavender oil on your hands and breathing the fragrance can be quite relieving of the pressure coming from the addiction. This is a method the shamans of the Amazon use to help combat addiction to cocaine and other scourges that people come to them to cure.

While prayer may not cure a severe habit or addiction all by itself, it can certainly support the process of overcoming it. The following prayer can be said in conjunction with other efforts to deal with the addiction.

Prayer to Clear Habits and Addictions

Begin by imagining the violet light flowing through your
body. Then pray.

Great Provider

I have been in the grip of something fierce

I thought I could manage it but I was
actually out of control

It was like a demon that arose inside me and
took over

It was managing me and not I it

It promised the world but it was stingy with
good feeling

I became a slave to it and let it be my master

This demon can kill me if I let it

I will not let it

I was meant for more important things

I am designed to be productive

To represent you in this worldly experience

I ask your help in shifting my direction

I thank you for your powerful support

I know you are assisting me and will not
abandon me

Together we will face this and together we
will change course

And every time I fall I will get up again

Every time I fall into failure
I become even more dedicated
To living free and independently
To be a slave to nothing
To be powerful and directed
Without time to waste
I will fight for my freedom and with you as
    my source
I am victorious
First in heart, then in mind, then in action
And through you I find that each day
I love myself more
I honor myself more
In your powerful name
I am victorious
I no longer yield one second's power to you,
    habit
You are no longer part of my life or my world
You will stay out
You have no power over me
I am loving myself now
I have purpose and meaning
I honor and respect myself now
I am victorious

OBSESSION AND COMPULSION

Some of us tend to obsess endlessly over what *did* happen, what *is* happening, and what *might* happen. This is certainly a pattern that I struggled with for a long time. We go over every nuance of every aspect of an event or situation in hopes of finding one more piece of clarity. Obsession and compulsion are defenses against the fear of being out of control because they give the illusion that everything is in order. When frightening or painful events occur, compulsion tries to undo them, to restore a sense of safety and security. If our house has been robbed once, then there may be an obsession and compulsion to lock every lock and check and recheck them over and over in order to provide a sense of security and stability.

Sometimes we have been subjected to hurtful treatment, perhaps from an alcoholic parent, and subconsciously we think that we must continue to deal with that alcoholic parent in order to show ourselves that we can survive. We keep obsessively marrying alcoholics and then divorcing them without realizing why. Doing and undoing will never help.

Being obsessive prevents the mind from relaxing because it must be constantly vigilant against the possibility that something bad might happen once again. The problem is that this is not an effective way to actually ward off danger. Obsession becomes dysfunctional and life becomes a dreary routine of checking and rechecking, doing and undoing, in an endless round of duty. The compulsion to repeat actions over and over is completely exhausting and will never actually provide security.

Unfortunately obsessing actually creates the opposite of safety or security because by pouring energy, focus, attention, and feeling into what we don't want we actually help to create our worst fears.

If you are willing to admit that you are behaving in an obsessive way, then prayer can be a significant help to you.

Prayer to Deal with Obsession and Compulsion

Great Spirit
When I have felt insecure and afraid
I thought that maybe I could be safe and
    secure
By doing something that relieves my fear
But I have found with hard experience
That it will never make me safe for good
My fear just kept coming back the same as
    before
I have tried to take care of my needs
But I have been more like a broken machine
Instead of turning to repetition to save me
I would rather turn to you
You are my safety and stability
You reside in every particle of me
The place I feel you the best
Is deep down in my chest
In the center of my heart where *I am*
This is where I feel safety

This where I know I will be cared for
And although I know there is no guarantee
That I will never be hurt again
I know you love me and I love you
And that is enough for me
I am truly safe
I am OK
I am

HANDLING DISCORD

For years in my life I was at the absolute mercy of negative emotions arising from difficult events and people. They would keep me up at night and harass my thoughts during the day, distracting me from my work and play. Working as a psychotherapist I noticed how much these negative emotions played havoc with others as well and no matter how much we talked about these things it did not help. Often I felt like the blind leading the blind. Not until I understood the shamanic power of decree was I able to get a handle on this kind of debilitating negativity.

Discord and disharmony are major obstacles to well-being and spiritual progress and these human-made limitations definitely cause us to feel separate and disconnected from Spirit. We need a method to deal with them fast or they pile up and cause us to lose faith and trust quickly.

Discord may come in the form of negative thoughts, a disharmonious and upset person who is blaming, judging and projecting, an unfortunate event or phone call, an argument or fight, a humiliation, a shameful memory, guilt, envy, jealousy, or any number of difficult emotional reactions. Fortunately there are several very effective techniques to banish these obstacles quickly and painlessly. In order to accomplish this you need to establish the usual heart opening technique that precedes effective prayer using the 'I Am' mantra. Once that has been established and you have closed the circuit by sending gratitude to essence, you may proceed with the shamanic decrees and commands.

Practice saying variations of these commands and find the one that works most effectively for you. The commands may sound simple but they do work amazingly well if you say them with firmness and intensity of feeling. You must speak with authority. You are entitled to command like this only after you have opened the doorway to your heart and contacted essence. Without essence backing you your commands will be weak and perhaps ineffective. Try it both ways and discover what works for you.

The most powerful commands given to the discord are these:

'Stop! You have no power; be gone!'

'You have no power over me. Get away.'

'Spirit, seize that thing and transmute it now.'

'Essence, flood that thing with a jet of violet light.'

'Essence, take my attention off this now!'

'Spirit, flood me with love and remove this thing.'

A Prayer to Halt Discord

Great Supplier and Provider
I have been pummeled by negative thoughts
I need your support and power backing me
    up right now
Take my attention off this now
Seize it and vanish it

Discord, you have no power over me
I command you to stop
Spirit, engulf me with a violet flame of
    protection and purity
Send it through my whole body
Especially through my heart and head
I know you never fail me

I am now clearing and feeling free
With your help I can be victorious
My thoughts and feelings accept only
    brilliant light
I am free and clear
I am in harmony

Part Five:

Getting On Track

UNDERSTANDING 'NOTHING'

It may seem strange to refer to Spirit as *nothing* or the *void* because this seems somehow to suggest that God has no value. This is not what is intended in the upcoming prayer. Certainly Spirit has infinite value yet, if the Creator is everything in the universe, the notion of God also includes 'not universe', 'void' or 'nothingness'. There is no aspect of existence or reality that the Creator is not. God must include every possibility, every dimension, even the background upon which the universe exists. The Hindu, Tibetan Buddhist, Christian, Sufi, indigenous shamans, and mystics everywhere understand and teach this fact. They know that God creates out of nothing and all the universes are continually dissolving back into the void millions of times every second only to be reinvented and recreated millions of times a second. The big bang is happening constantly and yet there is a storyline that we call 'official' history. So the universe is being recreated as we speak and, yes, there is evolution as well. In this respect shamans have no problem with creationism vs. evolution.

The feminine face of God is the great void and the

masculine face of Spirit is all manifested form. So the creator is continually showing masculine and feminine faces millions of times every second, winking the universe on and off in an ever present now point. This is symbolized in the ancient Taoist and shamanic Yin Yang sign, with black and white infinitely circling around each other within a mandala, each with a dot of the opposite color in its center.

This quality of the creator has very important implications. If the universe is being created millions of times a second in a kind of rapid series of big bang effects, and if it is dissolving completely for every time it is created, then there is constant potential for recreation or change in every instant. Nothing is fixed. It only appears to be fixed just as a movie film appears to be a fixed story as the many stills appear progressively on the screen. At any time an editor can introduce new stills or cut out old stills to change the storyline. Shamanically speaking, we as humans, co-creators with Spirit, can and do change the script through the power of prayer and decree.

HOLDING THE RIGHT PERSPECTIVE

Sometimes we have trouble believing that we are deserving of good things. We are taught that we have to earn blessings or that we must be punished for our constant wrongdoings. This is all quite foolish in the higher scheme of things because we are made in the image and likeness of Spirit. Spirit is the source of everything in the universe and that means that everything in the universe is Spirit and that we are made of Spirit or God Stuff. Our bodies are temples of Spirit, not just containers, but they are actually made of light that has Spirit as its source. If this is true, then we are due the same respect and honor that we show God. We are deserving of love, joy, opportunities, harmony, healing, and just about anything you can think of. It is not our little egos that deserve this, but the Spirit that we actually are, our essence selves. If we identify with ego, the self-important false personality, we are in trouble because ego will never be able to share the universe with God. It doesn't want to for selfish reasons. If we identify with Spirit then there is no problem with deserving and we can have all that we desire.

Prayer for the Right Perspective

*G*reat Spirit, *I am* your child, your creation
And because I hold this esteemed position
I deserve the best that life has to offer

If you are a king, then *I am* your prince
And if you are a queen, *I am* your princess
I am blessed with your name and your largess

Great Spirit, *I am* your loyal servant as well
And because I have the privilege to serve you
There is nothing I would not do in your
    service

Great Spirit, *I am* your witness experiencing
    your creation
And because you are everything, I participate
    in everything

And because you are also the great void,
    nothingness, there is no separate me

Great Spirit, You give me everything and
    then, like all forms, you absorb me back
    again into you
The only thing left is the light of awareness
    that you gave me for good

I thought I was in charge, but I was not in
    charge
You are in charge and I will do whatever you
    have in mind
Give me what you will and take away what
    you will

You know best and I accept your plan
And because I don't know everything
I will keep a 'don't know' mind

THE LORD'S PRAYER

The Lord's Prayer is one of the greatest prayers ever spoken.
The only problem with it is the archaic language that limits
understanding for our present generation. The Lord's Prayer
was first uttered in Aramaic, a rich language with many

nuances and undertones, but was then translated to Greek, a fixed language where it lost much meaning, and in turn to Latin, and finally to many other languages including English. Thus it might be a good idea to translate the Lord's Prayer into fresh words that can help to return it to its original Aramaic meaning. If you are attached to the old form and it has meaning for you then you may wish to continue to say it. This simple translation is only one out of many possibilities. Why not try your own hand at it?

The Lord's Prayer: alternative translation

Our father
Great Spirit, Creator, Source, Great Provider,
    Allah, Lord

Who art in heaven
Who is within us and everywhere right now

Hallowed be thy name
How infinitely great you are

Thy Kingdom come
Let your dream be realized

Thy will be done
Let your will be done

On Earth as it is in heaven
Here and now, everywhere in everything

Give us this day our daily bread
Thank you for all your blessings, all your
    resources

And forgive us our trespasses
Help us to forgive ourselves for mistakes and
    forgetfulness

As we forgive those who trespass against us
Help us to forgive those who forget their
    connection to Spirit

For thine is the kingdom, the power and the glory
For you are the great truth,

for ever and ever, Amen
for ever and ever, Amen

SLEEP

In this stressful world sometimes we have difficulty sleeping.
About half of all Americans have trouble sleeping at least a

couple of times a week and some have trouble all the time. Doctors prescribe sleeping pills but not only do they stop working after a time, they interrupt the deep regeneration that real sleep provides. While it is OK to take them on occasions such as international air travel or after surgery, they are not a good solution to sleeplessness in the long run. The reason that we can't get to sleep or why we wake up in the middle of the night is that we are disturbed by emotions that bring us back to physical waking or because our energetic balance has become disturbed due to bad habits. These feelings and imbalances distort our sleep cycles, influence our thoughts, and distort our sense of reality. They are a result of feeling cut off from our deepest source, Spirit. When these conditions persist then even a full eight hours of sleep doesn't suffice and we wake up more exhausted than when we went to bed. When we are truly connected to source, we get the sleep and the rest we need, even though that sleep cycle may be brief. Here is a prayer that can be said prior to sleeping. You may repeat it several times.

Prayer for Enhanced Sleeping

Spirit *I am* about to visit you
I look forward to traveling within your
    vastness
To rest deeply in your heart with my heart
As I lie here *I am* letting go of this outer dream
To enter into a deeper dream of knowing you
Restore me, revitalize me, heal me during my
    rest

Allow this breath to carry me to your depths
With each sigh I allow my body to slide into
   deeper rest
With each breath, my mind releases its activity
And I drift, I drift away, drift to you
To you, to dream, to integrate, to release
I sense my body relaxing
Deserving this time of tranquility
Organs quieting, eyelids heavy
Deeper, and deeper I go
Fingers and hands tingling
Feet tingling
As I withdraw
Withdraw
And sleep

A Prayer to Make Effective use of Sleep

Spirit, with your assistance and guidance
I *am* going to awaken in the morning full of
   vitality
I *am* awakening in the morning full of
   essence power
I *am* awakening to clear vision of my purpose

Every particle of my being is being charged
    while I sleep

Every cell is healing and returning to its
    original perfect state

As I sleep essence is charging me with its
    clear focus

Essence is guiding my thoughts and feelings

Spirit is carrying me to the temples of pure
    light

Where I may restore and remember what it is
    to awaken

Spirit is seeing that I remember what I
    learned upon awakening

During sleep every limitation and piece of
    baggage is released

All obstacles will spirit remove

Every doubt is banished

All sorrow leaves, I awake happy

And radiate goodness and power

When I awake, Spirit, show me the solutions
    to every problem

Clear my path and clarify my life task

Charge me with pure essence and Christ
    consciousness

Fill me with light and wisdom

Flood me with blessings so that when I
awaken
I am prepared to serve you, others, and myself

MASCULINE AND FEMININE

One of the greatest challenges we face as human beings is dealing with being a man or a woman and handling the opposite aspect within us. Historically there has been much mistreatment by men toward women and women toward men and a great mistrust has grown up for many around this pain. We need a great deal of help in getting back on track with love, honor, partnership, and cooperation between the sexes. In many parts of the world men dominate so completely that women still have few rights or freedoms. The world over, there is so much resentment toward men, that many women see them as wrong no matter what. Thus there is much work to do.

Not only do we sometimes distrust and mistreat the other sex, we often struggle with our own gender and don't feel comfortable within its skin. Coming to terms with being a man or a woman can be daunting at times. And even if we are comfortable with our own gender there is always the opposite gender within us to contend with. Our alternate side, masculine or feminine, can throw us into imbalance until we come to terms with it. Here are a couple of prayers that can help.

Prayer: On Being a Woman

*G*reat Spirit
I am woman
Reflecting the great feminine side of you
I am fortunate because
I am close to you in this way
I have your power to create, flowing through
    every particle of me
I share with all women this powerful gift of
    giving
And I don't mind the discomfort I bear for
    having this nature
The great basket of your love is my basket
Your powerful listening presence is my
    listening
The grand bowl of your potential is my bowl
Your great womb of creation is my womb
Where my greatest power lies
And I will give all of me in your name
And I will nurture and care for this world
Because that is what you do
And I will nurture and care for myself
Because I represent you
And I require honor and respect
Because I represent you
I will allow no abuse of myself or others

Because I represent you
And I will love my masculine side
Because that too is you
And I will love and respect men and children
Because you are in everyone
And I will support and uplift other women
Because you are in everyone
And I will treat animals and plants with
    respect
Because they too are you
And I will walk with nature and care for her
because that is the incubator you have given us

Prayer: On Being a Man

*G*reat Spirit
I am man
Reflecting the great male side of you
I am fortunate because
I am close to you this way
I have your power to intend and act
Flowing through every particle of me
And this is a huge responsibility that I am
    prepared to carry

I share with all men this powerful gift of
    intention and action

And I don't mind the challenges of carrying
    this nature

The powerful thrust of your ideas is my
    thrust

Your creative expression in form and word is
    my expression

Your dynamic power is my dynamism

Your guiding hand is my hand

And I will give all of me in your name

And I will take leadership for harmony and
    peace

Because that is what you do

And I will mentor those who look up to me

Because I represent you

And I will be generous and share my largess

Because I represent you

And I will act honorably and respectfully
    toward all

Because I represent you

And I will love and care for my feminine
    side,

Because that too is you

And I will behave honorably and respectfully
    toward women and children

Because you are in everyone

And I will cooperate with other men and
   walk in peace with them

Because you are in everyone

And I will treat animals and plants with
   respect

Because they too are you

And I will partner with nature and care for
   mother earth

Because that is the incubator you have given us

MASTERING EMOTION

Emotions give us a great range of experience and intensify the business of living but they can also be extremely hard to manage. Some people would rather repress their feelings because they find them too uncomfortable and messy to deal with. Others swing to the extreme polarities of emotion and struggle with bi-polar disorders. Artists learn to use emotion to express their creativity while others get caught in a quagmire of shifting feelings that utterly confuse them. According to the shamanic way, emotions are not easy to manage but they are such powerful tools that they must be mastered or they can create much havoc. Uncontrolled feelings are mostly destructive and overly controlled feelings rob you of the pleasure of living. As you have seen, emotions are what propel imagination into reality. They are the fuel of creativity and therefore they must be mastered.

Most people are utterly run by their feelings even if they think they are highly rational or intellectual. The Nazis thought they were completely rational in their final solution for the Jews but it is obvious they were motivated by negative emotions. Scientists often regard themselves as unmoved by feeling until you present evidence that threatens their favorite theories, then they show emotion galore.

Feelings need to be accessible and liberated but directed and disciplined. When you are attempting to meditate and trying to still your mind, it is feelings you are mostly struggling with. The feelings are driving your various thoughts, like how you are going to present your case at the meeting tomorrow or why someone didn't call you back on the phone. Feelings of concern, worry, hope, discouragement, anger, and attraction run these thoughts that circulate like a merry-go-round. These feelings are busy energizing thoughts and propelling them into manifestation. Instead of getting what you want you are often getting what you don't want.

Therefore it is necessary to be able to stop certain feelings from getting out of control. You have to learn to shut them down or they take over and run your life. You need to be able to allow the feelings that are helpful to flow into positive thoughts that result in manifesting what you want. This sounds simple but it is most assuredly not.

How to Manage your Feelings

First of all you need a shamanic mental technique that can stop certain feelings when they arise. Fighting or struggling is no good because that usually makes the feelings worse. Drinking or taking tranquilizers are only a temporary fix and often don't effectively stop the process at a subconscious level, so you just fool yourself into thinking that you have succeeded in stopping the feelings.

My shaman teachers taught me that everything consists of varying frequencies and that if you want to change something you must alter the frequency. Therefore one of the most effective shamanic devices you can use is color frequency because you can find a shade that is incompatible with the frequency of your feelings and subsequent thoughts. You need to select a color that is higher in frequency than the mental chatter you are having. This is relatively simple because most mental chatter is equivalent to gray, brown, or dull colors like olive green. The two colors that are most effective because of their high frequency are gold and violet. Send a jet of either of these colors up, starting at your feet and through your body, specifically through your heart and up through your head. You will be amazed at how quickly it stops the chatter. Of course the effect is temporary and soon it will begin again. So you must alter the frequency every time you have mental chatter that you don't find productive.

You can actually learn to practice this all day long and after awhile you will have revolutionized your feeling and thinking. Watch for your reactions to events. You will often see an immediate reaction in yourself that is not favorable. That is what you must learn to stop to gain mastery. With discipline it can be done.

Part Six:

Health and Healing

THE INNER SMILE

When life becomes sour, when our bodies do not function well, when events go wrong in our world, we have a tendency to frown and put on a long face directed especially at whatever body part we are feeling disagreeable about. Yet this attitude toward what hurts only makes it worse.

The Taoist shamans of ancient China, being experts in contemplating the power of nature, knew that the act of smiling could produce profoundly positive physiological affects on the body and on other matters as well. Therefore they created a powerful contemplation they called the inner smile. They knew that the Tao, their word for all that is, is in a perpetual state of smiling so to speak. They reasoned that if we smile along with the Tao, then we would be aligned with the most healing and powerful force in the universe. They knew that the results would be excellent and in fact they were. Today western research corroborates what the Taoists discovered and validates that they were absolutely right. Smiling and laughing do produce a great variety of positive effects on the body. However this does not mean that producing a fake smile to mask your real feelings toward another person is an effective strategy. The inner smile is effective because it begins with the critical 'inner' attitude; it is not just a cosmetic external facial expression that is designed to lie.

In order to practice the inner smile, here is what to do. Sit, stand, lie, or walk quietly and peacefully. Close your eyes two thirds of the way and produce and ineffable smile on your face similar to the Mona Lisa. Externally this is not a great big smile but a slight one. Then direct your attention toward whatever you have been having trouble with and produce a great big smile internally, but a slight smile externally. If you have been having a stomach ache or a pain in the kidney then direct your smile toward these areas. If you have been having difficulty with a person or a situation at work, direct your smile at them. Stay with each focus for a least several minutes.

If you have difficulty smiling because you are in a rotten mood then it helps to begin by focusing on something that truly tends to make you smile such as your dog, kitten, or nephew. Here is a part prayer, part exercise to facilitate your smiling contemplation on health.

Prayer: Smiling at My Body

I begin my smile with you Spirit
You are smiling back at me
Now I smile at you toes, feet, and ankles
You support me so well
I smile at you lower legs, bones, shins, and
   calves

You are powerful and strong
I smile at you knees, joints, tendons, and
    ligaments
You are most flexible and durable
I smile at you thighs and hamstrings
You are so reliable

I smile at you pelvis
You are perfectly aligned
I smile at you genitals
You are a source of great pleasure and
    connection
I smile at you bowels and rectum
You keep me so clean and light
I smile at you intestines
You absorb all that I need for health
I smile at you navel
A reservoir of power that you are
I smile at you diaphragm
You help me breathe so well

I smile at you liver on the right side
You keep my blood so clean
I flood you with sea green light to renew you
And smile at your happiness
I smile at you stomach

You digest my food so fine

I smile at you gall bladder

Bile you create for digestion

I smile at you heart

Great volumes of blood you pump

I flood you with vital red

To keep you happy and restored

I smile at you lungs, both left side and right

You breathe life into me and fill me with
    power

I flood you with platinum white

To clean you and relax you right

I smile at you pancreas

Hormones you deliver in balance

I flood you with bright yellow

To help you be mellow

I smile at my kidneys with adrenals perched
    atop

You are the source of health and vitality

I flood you with ink black

A color to bring you back

I smile at you spine

My nerves and messages you carry

I smile at you ribs and sternum

You keep my organs safe

I smile at you shoulders
So strong you are and so much you can carry
I smile at you upper arms
You are so good at holding and reaching
I smile at you elbows
You draw to me what is dear
I smile at you arms and wrists
So strong and durable are you
I smile at you hands and fingers
You express me so perfectly

I smile at you esophagus
The pipe for swallowing food
I smile at you throat and voice
You are my expressive choice
I smile at you jaw, teeth and gums
You taste and chew so well
I smile at you tongue
So many jobs you have
I smile at you nose and sinuses
Smelling and cleaning you do with kindness
I smile at you eyes
Seeing is such delight
I smile at you ears
Such music you allow me to hear
I smile at you brain

For with you I'm sane
And now I smile at all you lymph
You work so hard for me
I smile at all you muscles
Carry me to where you will
I smile at you nerve tree
And send light to every filament
I smile at all the rest
The whole miraculous temple
You hold Spirit to experience
This small part of creation

THE ORIGINAL TEMPLATE OF HEALTH

Our bodies are based on a blueprint, a perfect energetic pattern that produces a perfectly functioning body with optimal health. Even people born with disabilities have this perfect pattern behind their physical or mental challenges. Through accident, illness, age, and trauma our bodies fall into disrepair. This need not happen as great saints and shamans have demonstrated again and again. Powerful healers like Jesus are able to restore bodies to their original perfect pattern with a touch, a sound, a breath. The blind can see again, the deaf can hear, the lame can walk. Shipibo shamans of the Amazon heal by singing repairs into the energetic tapestry of the body based on this perfect blueprint. Knowing you have a perfect architectural design at the foundation of your health is very useful because it gives you something to return to. Here is a prayer dedicated to that aim.

Prayer for Perfect Health

*G*reat Spirit you have given me a magical body

I am most fortunate to have this wonderful vehicle to occupy

I didn't know that it had a design pattern

I didn't know how to take care of it

But now I know that it is always attempting to restore itself to perfection

I am healing

I am restoring to perfection

Every cell in my body is remembering its original design

Every cell of my body is restoring itself to perfection

Every cell of my body is bursting with vitality, youth, and vigor

I am healing

I am restoring to perfection

Every organ of my body is remembering its perfect structure

Every organ of my body is restoring to the original design

Every organ of my body is integrating
   perfectly with every other organ

I am healing

I am restoring to perfection

My skin knows its original design

I am feeling my skin restore itself to perfect
   health

My brain knows its original design

I am feeling my brain restore itself to perfect
   health

Every cell and structure in my brain is
   bursting with vitality and health

Every aspect of my throat is restoring and
   healing itself

My throat is perfect

My chest, lungs, and heart are all returning
   to perfection

They are bursting with health, energy, and
   vitality

My shoulders, arms, hands, and fingers are
   great

They are returning to their original perfection

My liver, adrenals, and kidneys are returning
   to optimal health

Every cell is restoring itself and radiating
   light and energy

My thyroid and thymus are totally healthy

All the cells are turning young and energetic

My stomach, pancreas, and gallbladder are healing

They are filled with vitality and perfection

My intestines, bladder, and rectum are restoring to total health

Every cell and fiber of them are vitalizing and healing

My genitals and reproductive organs are returning to their perfect state

They are restoring to complete health and vitality

My pelvis, hip joints and thighs are restoring themselves

Every aspect of them is returning to its original perfection

My knee joints, lower legs, ankles, and feet are rejuvenating

All their parts are turning young again

They are working perfectly like their original design

My whole body is returning to a state of perfection

I am returning to my original perfect design and blueprint

I am whole

I am restored

I am healed

Prayer for Healing Arthritis

I thought I had stiff joints
I thought I could not bend
I thought I was like a board
With no flex and mend
But now I feel Spirit flow
Through every particle and atom
Energy flows, warm and pink
And swelling begins to shrink
I am restoring these joints
To their original flexibility
I am mending these joints
To their original design points
Pain fades away
And light takes its place
I am restructuring my joints
Spirit within me anoints
To flow freely and with grace
In a dance of vitality

VOICE AND EXPRESSION

Voice is more than the sounds we make with our throats. Voice is who we are and how we express this essence. Voice is our expression through posture, gesture, intonation, cadence, intensity, and the fluidity of our energy in motion. Voice is what we don't say as well as how well we speak our truth. Voice is what people get from us, how they are inspired and influenced by us even when we are not physically present.

Shamanically speaking voice is a great power and yet it is so often distorted and stifled. When we are young and wish to express who we are, sometimes no one is listening. Sometimes people around us are too busy, too stressed, or threatened by us and they squash our voice. Our voices still want to be heard but now they must conform to someone else's standard or perfect pictures of what we must say and how we must say it. Without even realizing it we may speak another's words instead of our own truth. So by the time we are adults our voices may have grown weak, hoarse, strained, deceitful, strident, judgmental, whiny, or harsh.

Most of us need healing around our self-expression. We need help getting rid of the doubts, the anger, the distortions, and the fear about expressing who we really are. Then our voices may ring out clearly and powerfully. Prayer can help, as always.

Prayer for Healing Voice and Expression

Creator
You gave me a voice
You gave me the means to express myself

I have used my voice for many things

Not always lovingly or for the most good

Sometimes I lied to keep from getting caught

Sometimes I laughed at someone instead of
with them

Sometimes I exaggerated to make myself look
better

Sometimes I spoke in anger and yelled at
another

Sometimes I used my voice against myself

I attacked myself

Trashed myself

Apologized endlessly for myself

These are not ways I choose to use my voice
any longer

You created my voice

It is your voice for you to speak through me

You gave me uniqueness

You gave me special talents

You gave me a voice to let the world know I
am here

When *I am* aligned with you

My voice is filled with power

With light

With influence

My voice is to nurture with

My voice is to lead with

My voice is to show compassion for
My voice is to speak with love to
My voice is to delight others with
My voice is to entertain with
My voice is to connect with others
My voice is to connect with you
My voice is your voice
Spirit help me to always remember
Thank you for giving me my real voice
And help me to express with courage

The Immune System

Our way of life poses great challenges for our immune systems. Toxins, pesticides, food additives, chemical compounds in products, vaccines and medications can all play havoc with our bodies' protection system. The thymus gland located below the thyroid gland under the throat is central to the body's immune system. This gland in infants is proportionally huge and takes up most of the upper chest. By the time we are adults it has shrunk down proportionally to a small size. The thymus is often overwhelmed with what it has to deal with and exhausts itself by middle age due to constant stress and a toxic environment. There is an exercise that can support the thymus and increase the effectiveness of your immune system.

The Dine people (Navajo) of the south-western part of the

United States, the Chinese Taoists, and most shamans I have met in other traditions understand the importance of speaking directly to the organs of the body to re-integrate them with the rest of the body. Particular organs can become isolated, unhappy and cut off, resulting in their malfunctioning or becoming diseased. Talking to them acknowledges them, gives them positive attention, and makes them feel loved. They are more likely to heal in response to being addressed directly and with love.

Sit quietly and locate your thymus gland with the fingers of either hand. Find the V cleft in your throat and go down a couple of inches and you should be there. Gently touch your fingers to that location and let them rest there. Do not use your fingers to push energy into your thymus, rather let your thymus gland become aware of the helping fingers beckoning them just outside the skin. Get the idea that your thymus gland is so glad to be attended to that it readily reaches out for your fingers. Remember your fingers gently beckon and ever so slightly pull but do not actually do anything. Now focus on the *I am* point in your heart and feel yourself being there. The secret is to create a communication of love with your thymus gland. When it experiences this love it will automatically begin to heal itself in whatever way is necessary. (You can do this for any organ of the body). This process is very brief, usually under a minute and possibly just a few seconds. Now lower your hand and you are done. Drink plenty of fluids to support its cleansing.

If you wish you can say the following prayer while holding your fingers in the position mentioned above.

Prayer for Thymus Gland Healing

Thymus gland

Thank you for the tremendous job you have done
  Serving me all these years

Thank you for protecting me from diseases

Thank you for fighting off maladies
  Unfriendly viruses and bacteria

Your job is complex and you must
    orchestrate so much

You are like a general commanding huge
    armies of cells

You work hard and loyally for me twenty-four
    hours a day

It is nothing short of miraculous what you
    accomplish

I am glad of your help

I am sorry if I have neglected to thank you
    before

I wish you well and I want you to be happy

I want you to be fully in communication

With all other parts of me

I love you and I know you must love me
    given your record

I am happy to talk to you

I am glad you are with me

Supporting me, healing me, caring for me

A Prayer to Clear all Traces of Cancer

Spirit

The doctors say I have cancer

I have had symptoms that they diagnosed

It means there appears to be something very
   wrong in my body

I have many choices facing me about
   treatments and methods

I have felt a bit overwhelmed

Being told I have cancer was frightening to
   me

But whatever the reasons and whatever the
   symptoms

I still have you

You are my awareness, my aliveness, my
   source

The source of my warmth and vitality

You are the source of my dreams

I am alive

I am conscious

I am connected with you

You are here humming away deep in my heart

I feel your warmth

I feel your power

You are what I need

I am focusing on you, my source, with every

second I have

I feel you radiating out from my heart

And flooding my body with violet light

A beautiful violet flame

The flame consumes all doubt and distortion

In my thoughts, in my feelings, in my intent

And as all the doubt burns up in the violet
flame

I feel strength, a powerful force

Emanating from my heart

And now a powerful gold light floods
outward

To every cell, to every atom of every cell

Clearing, balancing, harmonizing

Diseased cells and tissue are carried away

Disposed of in the proper way

There is no limit to the golden light

I feel my heart so warm

I feel you there, *I am* there

I am my own healing

I am healed

I am well

My healthy cells are strong and powerful

I am healed

I am well

I am completely whole

EXHAUSTION

For shamans, to be exhausted requires a great deal of energy. Exhaustion is an unnatural condition of being cut off from the great source of vitality and power within essence. To maintain this state of separation requires more energy that only contributes to the state of exhaustion. The short-term solution is of course rest but the long-term solution is to restore the connection to essence and thus to Spirit. This prayer is aimed at that.

Prayer for Revitalizing

*C*reator

I have allowed myself to feel very tired

I seem to have run out of energy

I *am* taking care of myself now and I *am* resting deeply

I *am* also reestablishing my connection with you

I *am* feeling your constant source deep in my heart

I *am* feeling you there humming without ceasing

Although the rest of me felt run down

When I feel you in my heart you are strong and vital as ever

I *am* feeling this warm sense of aliveness

Spreading slowly outward
Spreading like a warm glow of light
Sending love and nurturing
Sending confidence radiating outward
And as *I am* deeply resting
I am renewing my connection with you
And as *I am* deeply resting
I am finding my source in you
And as *I am* deeply resting
I am feeling your love for me pouring forth
And as *I am* deeply resting
Your light radiates out throughout my body
Restoring, renewing, revitalizing
I am restored
I am renewed
I am revitalized
I am healed
I am your strength
I am your love
I am rested

BREATHING

In the shamanic world breathing is the way we keep rhythm with the universe. We take in our world, process it inside, and then breathe out what is inside to mix with the world. Standing in a meadow in the spring we breathe the fresh clear air and sigh with great satisfaction. At the ocean we breathe salty air and in the mountains the cold clear scent of pine.

Our breath not only oxygenates our blood but it carries our words and allows us to taste and smell the world. Breath is quite simply life.

When we have intense emotions or disturbing thoughts our cycle of breathing is interrupted. At times of deep fear we hold our breath awaiting the outcome of events. Anger causes heaving and sadness delivers sobs. Laughter helps us to breathe deeply.

Sometimes substances are so irritating to our noses and lungs that they create a huge interference in our breathing. We get allergies and asthma and life can become miserable. When we get colds or chest infections congestion sets in and breathing becomes hard work. Nothing is quite so satisfying in life as clear, uninterrupted, even breathing. This becomes quite evident when we have lost it for a while.

The following is a shamanic prayer dedicated to the breath. Take your time with it and monitor your breathing as you say the prayer. Use this prayer as a tool to work with your breathing.

Prayer for Lungs

I am breathing
I am breathing
I am breathing in Spirit
I am breathing clearly with Spirit
I am breathing in and out
I am breathing deeply
I am breathing around my heart
I am breathing behind my heart
I am breathing life and vitality into me
I am breathing
I am breathing
I am breathing bright platinum white
My lungs are glowing platinum white
My lungs are expanding
I am breathing life
I am breathing love
I am breathing vitality
I am breathing bright platinum white
My lungs are glowing platinum white
My lungs are surrounding my heart
I am breathing into my heart
My heart is opening
My heart is welcoming Spirit
I feel my diaphragm moving with each b

My breath goes deeper
Down into my abdomen
My breath is going deeper into my abdomen
I am breathing Spirit deep into me
My breath is awakening Spirit in me
I am glowing
I am glowing with light
I am breathing
I am breathing
Deep, deep, deep
I am breathing Spirit
I am breathing light
I am breathing love
I am breathing

Part Seven:

Developing Virtues

Wisdom

Information is not wisdom, nor is simply having knowledge. You can have knowledge of a minefield and yet unwisely walk into it. Wisdom is something that is not limited to the workings of the brain. You can be exceptionally smart and yet not be wise, as many a criminal can attest. So what is wisdom? Wisdom is something you accumulate over a long gradual life education. Wisdom is the ability to see the big picture and understand what you are seeing in the context of what is best for the greatest good. Wisdom implies developed values, perceiving in a way that others have not yet been able to penetrate. That is why people go to a wise person for assistance.

A wise person always has an open heart because that is where wisdom resides, yet wisdom is not emotional or sentimental. A wise person is kind yet not overly protective; understanding yet not fawning; loving yet capable of being ruthlessly truthful. A wise person does not avoid your eyes when listening. A wise person does more listening than speaking. Wisdom may be spoken by the young and lost on the elderly. Most of all, a wise person has a deep connection to Spirit and understands that they know very little in the large scheme of things.

Prayer for Wisdom

Great Spirit

I have learned much during my life so far

I know and understand how to do many
    things

Thank you for making me intelligent

Thank you for giving me the opportunities to
    learn

Thank you for all the things you have
    exposed me to

I know that being intelligent doesn't make
    me wise

Nor does being educated in a conventional
    way

I desire to be a wise person in addition to
    being smart

I desire to be wise in all ways as you are

Thank you for giving me the opportunity to
    become wise

Thank you for helping me to listen more

To watch more

To withhold my judgment longer

To speak the truth as I know it with courage

Thank you Great Spirit for access to wise
people

Thank you for providing me with nature to
learn from

Thank you for helping me to remain silent
for long periods of time

So that I can contemplate and hear you
speak to me

I know that wisdom does not come all at
once

I am listening

I will listen

I am becoming wise

Because you are all wise

And you are my source

You are within me

I have access to you at all times

I realize from my vantage point

That I know very little

Yet you are teaching me daily about what has
heart and meaning

Great Spirit I open my heart to you

I open my heart to experience

Thank you for helping me to withhold
judgment

To see with clarity

To understand without confusion
To perceive with accuracy
To be insightful and filled with awareness
Thank you for making me a wise person
So that I may be generous and serve
So that I may make a contribution
And fulfill my life task work
Yes, with you in me, *I am* wise

ABOUT LOVE

There is no more important human experience than to love and be loved. Although affection comes naturally as it does to all mammals, the ability to truly love must be cultivated and learned over a long period of time. Too often our primitive attempts to love are actually simply a need for affection based on conditions. We are affectionate with those who meet our conditions. 'If you give me things I will love you'; 'If you do as I say I will love you'; 'If you are nice to me I will love you.' Eventually after many difficult lessons we learn to love unconditionally but this takes much experience and a great deal of effort.

A parallel challenge is to learn to love yourself unconditionally as well. This is harder yet because to do so we must get past all the self-loathing, self-deprecation, low self-esteem, and lack of forgiveness for not being perfect.

One important aspect of loving yourself is the experience

of knowing that you are loved and allowing that love to penetrate from the outside in, or to emerge from the inside out. There is a kind of 'chicken or egg' question to all this. What comes first – learning to love yourself or learning to love others? Learning to let love in or learning to love yourself? The only way we can truly learn to love is to be loved first because this is how we learn about love. People and animals who have been shown no love are often mean, ruthless, angry, or unresponsive. Yet, even if we haven't been shown love at a young age it is possible to become a loving person. In order for this to happen it is necessary to recognize at the deepest levels that love is the substance of creation and is therefore fueling every particle of the universe. Love truly is inside of consciousness.

If this is true how can it be that at times we feel unloved? Sometimes we are so close to something that we fail to see it just like the proverbial nose on our face. We are busy looking past it and therefore cannot find it. We are in a state of ignorance or illusion believing that love is something to find externally. It certainly can feel that way to the body that wants visibly and tangible signs of affection. Yet ultimately love is found at the very core of awareness and to discover it we have to learn to look within. That is not something that we are taught to do nor is it something that gratifies us at first.

Shamanically speaking, the spiritual colors of love are pink and ruby. If you so choose you can imagine flooding yourself, especially your heart, with these colors while you pray. That way your shamanic prayer will become much more powerful.

Here is a prayer that focuses on finding where love is to be found.

Prayer to Cultivate Love

Spirit, sometimes I have felt completely
    alone

At times I didn't recognize that *I am* loved

On occasions I felt unloved and I haven't felt
    loving toward others

I felt cut off

I thought, maybe I needed to do something
    different to find love

Perhaps I needed to change my way of doing
    things

Or maybe I needed to find new people to
    love me

Then I laugh and realize how silly this is

There is nothing I need to change to
    experience love

I am floating on a bed of love

You are my source at this very moment

And if I tune in and feel my aliveness

Especially in my chest

I feel a glow, I feel a warmth

That is deep within me

You fill every space with your intent to create

And that intent is fueled by the most
    profound love

You generously create and then bestow free will

You give us the choice to forget about you

You give us the choice to forget about love
and connection

When I felt separate I couldn't feel love

When I feel connected I know love is all
around

Love is the answer, you are the source

I am loving

I am loved

Yes, I'm home again

And if I forget in five minutes

It doesn't mean that love is not here

Love will still be all around me and in me

And I will need to remember again and again

Until I can no longer forget

I am loving

I am loved

DEATH

Death terrifies us even if it comes as relief from suffering or pain. Many of us are afraid to talk about death or we pretend it will not happen to us. We like to hide it so that it does not touch us too closely with its finality. Death is all around yet it is the great unknown, a true mystery of the infinite. There are no survivors on this planet, at least not that we know of or have met. Death comes for each one of us at an unannounced date. We cannot control death unless we commit suicide and even then sometimes we botch the job. So nothing is certain about death but death itself.

Parts of us die and slough off every day but we do not mourn those dead cells. We shower and are glad to get rid of them, but not so the whole body. That loss is too much for most of us. Yet, death is no different from essence taking a shower to get rid of old coverings. Essence need not take the body along at the end of life just as we do not put on shoes or clothes that have grown tattered or too small for what we have become.

Mystics and shamans say that death can be so much easier if we get used to the idea early in life. 'Pray for a good death' they say. Here is a prayer for a good death.

Prayer for a Good Death

Spirit you create me and take me away
    many times a second
So quickly does this happen that I take no
    notice
Yet contemplating going away for good is scary
What will I become?
Will there still be a me that knows who I *am*?
And what me will that be?
What if I just cease to be?
Or worse what if I can still be aware but
    tortured forever?

Ah, but parts of me are dying as I speak
And parts of me are being born
I am never the same minute to minute
So why should it be any different when I
    leave this body?
I will leave as I came in
And I will be born anew

Spirit I know you will be with me when my
    body's end comes
I know you will guide me and show me what
    to do
So that I will not be frightened
You will surround me with people who love
    me
Either in spirit or in person
You will bestow calmness and tranquility on
    me
And you will show me what I have learned
    and where *I am* going
I will graduate with honor and blessings
And I will experience your love coming
    through me
 Exquisitely, sweetly, pervasively
And I will bless all those I leave behind for a
    short time
And I will be missed but more importantly,

I will be gladly sent along, because I will
    have earned my transition
And my loved ones will rejoice at my
    memory
Because in my short lifetime I will have made
    a difference
And I will die with smile on my face

ABOUT SEX

People are seldom neutral about sex. Either they are starving
for it, feeling guilty over it, experiencing shame about it, hating
it, wanting it with someone new, bored with it, stressed about
it, trying to ignore it, warding it off, too exhausted for it, or
indulging in it excessively. Very few people say they have the
perfect sex life and if they do it seldom lasts all their lives
because of illness, travel, work, death, and stress. Sex is not a
neutral thing but is tied up with self-esteem, health, self-image,
partnership, temporary feelings, and a host of other influences.
The bottom line is that most people wish they had a better relationship with sex just as they wish they had a better
relationship with their bodies.

Many people don't feel comfortable praying about sex
because they feel ashamed to think about sex while talking to
God, but this is absurd. Spirit created sex and it is an important
part of healthy life. Of course God knows all about sex and of
course it is right to talk to Spirit about sex. After all Spirit is
combining and recombining to become 'one' constantly.

Cross-culturally shamans consider sexual energy to be the foundation of personal power. They discipline themselves to build up this store of energy so they can transmute it for healing and awakening to wisdom. For them sexual energy is a sacred trust not to be squandered by either greed or shame. Sexual energy is what powers their dreaming and their magical flights for discovery of knowledge and tools of transformation.

So here is a little shamanic prayer about sexual energy.

A Prayer for Balanced Sexuality

Spirit, thank you for giving me my body.
Thank you for making my body an
    experience of great pleasure
Thank you for making me a sexual being
And thank you for helping me express my
    sexuality appropriately
Thank you for helping me to be satisfied
With how my sex life ebbs and flows
My sexuality has its tides, its peaks and its
    valleys
Thank you for helping me to understand this
And relax in the face of it
Thank you for helping me to know that
    desire is natural
And that sexual expression can be divine
Let me share this pleasure and
    communication with the right person

Let us delight in experiencing each other's
bodies

And let this sharing always be with one who
is my equal

With one who consents and has the maturity
to know what they want

Let this person delight in me, and I in them

And if I be alone, let me express my sexuality
in a way most fitting

So that you are honored and *I am* pleased

And nature takes its course

I am a sexual being

I am a beautiful sexual being

May I express my sexuality completely
naturally

As does everything in nature

FORGIVENESS

Forgiving those who hurt us or whom we imagine have harmed
us, is a profound challenge. We are afraid at the deepest levels
that if we forgive the other person they will be off the hook and
won't have to pay for what they did. Even worse we feel that
perhaps they will hurt us all over again. We worry that perhaps
if we forgive others we will once again make ourselves
vulnerable, so withholding forgiveness makes us ever vigilant.

There is a difference between forgiving and being naïve. We can forgive others while still learning to set boundaries and take care of ourselves. We might say, 'I forgive you your debt but never ask me for money again.'

Carrying blame and resentment against others is a poison that none of us can afford. We are the people who are most hurt by a lack of forgiveness. So, little by little, we must learn to forgive because we are made to be like the creator and the creator forgives all.

Forgiving ourselves for our own mistakes can be even harder than forgiving others. Most of us are very hard on ourselves and we need help allowing forgiveness in. Holding ourselves hostage because of our mistakes is horrifically destructive and can result in self-punishing cancers, accidents, losses in business and failures in relationships. Thus we must learn to forgive ourselves even if what we have done has been extremely harsh and destructive. Again we are afraid that if we let ourselves off the hook, we will just repeat the offense, so withholding forgiveness is supposed to keep us in line. But from a shamanic point of view lack of forgiveness does not make us into better human beings. Actually indulging in withholding forgiveness simply makes us stuck, deeply miserable, and results in a horrible power loss. Not forgiving is like constipation, nothing flows and everything is stopped up. When we no longer flow, we become unhealthy, and that is not fun for essence.

Once again we must ask, 'Who are we not to forgive ourselves when the Creator forgives all immediately?' Essence is invested in us moving on because it knows that is the road to happiness and eventual fulfillment. Spirit wants to experience fulfillment through each of us. Spirit wants all of us to come home to celebrate reunion with the infinite.

As mentioned elsewhere, the color violet is the color of for-giveness. This color is a frequency that is incompatible with blame or judgment. While you pray you may wish to imagine dousing yourself with the violet color or imagine a violet flame consuming your body. This is like turbo-charging your prayer.

Here is a shamanic prayer to help with forgiveness.

Prayer for Forgiveness

Great Spirit I dreamed I had been used and
    abused

I believed that I was victimized unjustly

I believed that I was taken advantage of and
    directly undermined

What I have been through felt unfair

I haven't wanted to forgive

Because I have held onto anger and
    resentment

I thought they should pay for what they did
    to me

But who made me the judge and jury

Who appointed me the one to exact revenge

This is not my job

You have told me to forgive seven times
    seven

That is so hard for me

But I can forgive this time with your support

You are the great forgiver

You hold no grudges

You want only that we advance

You made us to keep our own accounts

And all shall be accounted for and paid up

So who am I to control from my limited
perspective

I am grateful for your help in forgiving

I am forgiving

I am completely forgiven

Allow me to release all blame and judgment

And may I strengthen in character and
compassion

May I forget revenge immediately

May I move forward having learned whatever
is necessary

That *I am* forgiving

And *I am* forgiven completely

COURAGE

When I was a child I lacked confidence and was a complete
coward when it came to dealing with other people. I was
terribly shy and would hide in the bathroom when my parents
had visitors. This lack of courage translated into many events of
my life. As a young person I often lacked the courage to tell the

truth and lied to cover a mistake. One time I stayed home sick with a fever and my parents left me with a thermometer so that I could take my temperature. They warned me not to break the thermometer. Naturally I dropped it and broke it. So when they came home I couldn't face telling them. I told them I lost it. Finally my dad got the truth out of me by asking where I dropped it. Then I told him, much embarrassed.

Life on this planet poses such challenges that it takes a lot of courage just to grow up and even more to deal with whatever comes up in adult life. Many people think that fear is the enemy of courage but it is not so. Fear exists whether we are courageous or not. The most courageous people still feel fear, they just don't let it stop them from taking the action required at the moment of risk. This is a central tenet of the shamanic way. Courage then is not the absence of fear nor is it might or aggression. Courage can be quiet protest or humble dedication in the face of overwhelming odds.

Nor is courage a concept or a rational conclusion, rather it comes spontaneously from an open heart. The most courageous people are vulnerable people who are in touch with their humanity. They are open-hearted enough to be generous even at great risk to their own well-being. They seek the higher good and they put their own safety on the line for it. They can only do this if they have purpose and meaning in their lives. This is what I learned from Don Guadalupe.

Prayer for Courage

*G*reat Spirit

You are my source of courage

You pour confidence through me

So that I may fill the vacuum of leadership

You support me in speaking out for peace

You strengthen me in speaking out for
compassion

You guide me in questing cooperation

You are giving me the gift of leadership

At a time most crucial

I am a powerful leader

To help guide the way

For all those fearful and floundering

In such a challenging time

You are giving me the gift of being a mentor

For others who need a model for maturity

I am an excellent role model

I walk my talk and live my truth

With your guidance and support

To help show the frightened ones how to be

You are giving me the gift of courage

To face whatever forces of ignorance arise

I am filled with courage

You are giving me the gift of courage

To face the challenges coming
I am

BEAUTY

Wherever and whenever you witness beauty you are seeing with the eyes of essence. Noticing beauty around you is intensely healing for you and others. This is one of the reasons that people bring beautiful flowers to people in hospital who are recovering from an accident or illness. When you see ugliness you are seeing the product of false personality made manifest in the world and in a way you are contributing to that ugliness. A garbage dump is such a product. You can increase the frequency that you see beauty in your environment not just by moving to a more lovely location but by connecting more with your own essence. You can connect with Spirit through the *I Am* point in your heart. You will then see more beauty in the people all around you and you will definitely see more beauty in the mirror. Seeing beauty is seeing with a higher frequency. In a way that is difficult to explain, when you see beauty in something or someone you actually make what you see more beautiful. Others will be able to see it too. That is why someone who is loved will seem more attractive to others as well.

My Huichol teacher Don Guadalupe taught me a great deal about the power of beauty and how to work with it. He explained that his people dress in vivid gorgeous colors to show honor and respect to the Creator who made human beings to resemble flowers. He taught me to visualize beautiful flowers on the altar throughout all-night healing ceremonies in the stark desert of central Mexico. According to him, beauty had a great power to heal and draw benefits from Spirit and the more vivid the colors, shapes, and forms the greater the overall results. My experience taught me the truth of his words.

A Prayer to Enhance Beauty

Creator
You are the source of all beauty in this
   universe
You are beautiful and you create everything
   out of yourself
So of course there is beauty in everything
Sometimes I forgot to look for the beauty
And saw only what was ugly
Because my thoughts were ugly
I missed my opportunity when I did that
Now I see there is beauty in everything
And when I look for beauty
I create beauty just like you
And everything becomes more beautiful
You are beautiful
So I am beautiful too
I see beauty in everything
The beauty I see comes back to me

In a powerful circle of increase
The more beauty I see
The more beauty there is
What a power beauty has

Part Eight:

Dealing with Fears

Victimization

When my parents got angry with me they could lose their tempers and get a little rough. Later when the moment passed and they were calm they would smile and try to engage me in conversation. I was so hurt I refused to make eye contact, smile or interact with them. I felt so victimized I wanted to punish them for hurting me. I didn't want to give in and make it seem like spanking and slapping me was OK. Perhaps my feelings were understandable for a child but this is not the way an adult should behave.

From a shaman's perspective one of our greatest obstacles is the tendency to feel sorry for ourselves over what happens in life. Feeling like a victim is a cause for blaming others and seeing them as predators and victimizers. By doing so we empower them with our fears to harm us. This is both a way of undermining ourselves and energizing the most primitive instincts of others so no one wins. To erase victimization is a discipline. We can't afford to allow our thoughts to stray there even briefly and although it may seem unrealistic at times, there is a tried and true method of dissolving victimization. The method is actually an ancient one and has been taught in many mystery schools throughout the ages.

The antidote for martyrdom is to see yourself as cause rather than effect. Now it is important to understand that seeing yourself as cause does not mean that you are to blame. It simply means that you are responsible for what you experience. Remember, the word responsible means 'response able', able to respond. Even that may be a hard concept to swallow while you are doing the contemplation below. Here I am not talking about your everyday personality or ego being the cause but rather your deeper more expansive self, your essence. What you want to do is reinforce your identification with your essence and relax your identification with your ego or false self because that is just a pawn in life. If you identify with it you are in deep trouble.

Find a place where you can sit, stand, or walk without interruption for a little while. Let anything you see, hear, feel, think, or experience be grist for the mill. The contemplation practice goes something like this:

Contemplation on Responsibility

I am responsible for what I see because I am the one seeing it.

I am responsible for what I hear because I am the one hearing it.

I am responsible for what I feel because I am the one feeling it.

I am responsible for my reaction because I am the one reacting.

I am responsible for what I touch because I
am the one touching.

I am responsible for my thoughts because I
am the one thinking.

I am responsible for my actions because I am
the one acting.

I am responsible for my interpretation
because I am the one interpreting.

I am responsible for my assumptions because
I am the one assuming.

I am responsible for my anger because I am
the one who is angry.

I am responsible for my sadness because I
am the one who is sad.

I am responsible for my happiness because I
am the one who is happy.

I am responsible for my playfulness because I
am the one who is playful.

I am responsible for my loss because I am
the one experiencing loss.

I am responsible for my worry because I am
the one worrying.

I am responsible for my healing because I am
the one being healed.

I am responsible for my hopes and dreams
because I am their source.

I am responsible for my prayers because I am
the one praying.

I *am* responsible for my pain because I am
the one in pain.

I *am* responsible for my self realization
because this is my life.

I *am* responsible to become enlightened
because this is my destiny.

I *am* responsible for being one who
experiences life because this is my
experience.

I *am* responsible for being God's
representative because I am a co-creator.

I *am* responsible for my talents because they
are my talents.

I *am* responsible for my body because it
belongs to me.

I *am* responsible for illness because it is my
experience.

I *am* responsible for my healing because it is
my experience to heal.

And so on. You get the idea. Continue this exhaustively on a
regular basis and gradually you will be liberated from victimization. Don't be surprised if you feel many emotions arise
while doing this. Anger, outrage, sadness, tears, relief, and
empowering feelings are all common reactions. Just note them
and continue the contemplation without indulging your
feelings.

ARROGANCE AND SELF-CONSCIOUSNESS

On this planet with six and one half billion people it is easy to feel small and overlooked. So many of us, due to insecurity, try to put on an important façade in hopes that we will stand out from the crowd to be given special attention and honor. What we want is to feel special, loved, and attended to. In shamanic terms this tendency toward self-importance becomes a massive obstacle to our freedom because as long as we are enslaved by this need we are in prison. Therefore for a shaman, self-importance must be banished no matter how hard the path. Sometimes shamans and spiritual teachers use fairly brutal methods to rid their apprentices of this scourge. Fortunately Don Guadalupe and my other teachers did not follow these methods but taught with compassion and subtlety as a way to turn me away from my own self-importance.

The wish to be special often comes from a childhood where love was conditional and where we needed to prove ourselves in order to be loved. Often this challenge came with criticism, judgment, and shaming if we did not perform well. These wounds can persist into adult life and cause no end of havoc as we build protective shells and try to beat everyone else for attention. We hide vulnerability, avoid intimacy, and spend a great deal of time thinking and worrying about our own per-formance and the result is the pain of self-consciousness, false pride, and loneliness. I remember the futility of working hard to earn money for my first car so I could impress the girls in high school. Being only a used pea-green Volkswagen it was hardly impressive. The car was not a substitute for real confidence and I knew it deep inside.

Fortunately there is a cure for arrogance and self-consciousness and that is to remember who we are on a shamanic spiritual level. With that recognition all false pretense falls away and we know who we are once again. Here is a prayer to enhance that process.

Prayer to Erase Arrogance and Self-Consciousness

Great Spirit

I have been confused

I have suffered shame because I forgot who I
was

I thought I was a separate self

Alone against the world

I thought I had to survive by performing well

For others to approve

I thought I had to survive by protecting
myself

Against others' painful jabs

I criticized others because I was once
criticized

I judged because I was once judged

I disparaged because others once disparaged
me

I acted self-righteous because I have been
confused

I worried about how I looked because I
might not be up to par

I worried about how people thought of me

I thought they would be harsh

Because I have been confused about who I
am

I was afraid to look at myself because I
would attack myself

I was afraid to show my deeper self

Because I thought I would be taken
advantage of

I was afraid of intimacy

Because I was afraid I would look foolish

I was afraid to be vulnerable because I
thought I would be hurt

I was afraid of trying

Because I thought I would be judged

I wanted everyone to admire me because I
didn't admire myself

I wanted everyone to notice me

Because I was afraid I would be ignored

I wanted to be special and important

Because I thought I would be overlooked

Now I know that all these worries were just
dreams

Illusions of my mind

There is no me that has to be propped up

Only a spiritual being on life's journey

Attempting to wake me up

Now that I know this false self can never find
the truth

I am realizing that only essence holds my
truth

I am a divine being playing the human game

I am God's child, always loved, ever valued

I am a being with a contribution to make

I look to see how I can serve

Never again to lose my nerve

I am confident

I am powerful

I am safe revealing who *I am*

I am God's child, always loved, ever valued

I am perfect just the way I am

Bumbling and all

No need for being special when I have a job
to do

No need for shame, no need for protection

I am God's creation, always loved, always
valued

IMPATIENCE

Impatience is the scourge of modern life. The fast pace just keeps getting faster and with it stress rises, health suffers, and we fall away from presence. When we are pushed to achieve more, faster, at every turn we eventually fall out of rhythm with our deeper selves. We become accident-prone, harrassed, and basically unhappy. Relationships suffer, parenting becomes poorer, and we become disappointed in ourselves. We actually run out of patience with ourselves and become irritated, even angry most of the time. What suffers most is our spiritual lives and sense of deep meaning about why we are here and what our lives are about. This is obviously no way to live. What we need is to slow down and reconnect with who we are and what our purpose is. The first order of business is to slow down before praying.

Impatience has no place in the shaman's world. Indigenous shamans have a totally different concept of time and for them an all-night healing ceremony is the most natural process in the world. More often than not their ceremonies last days on end and require vigorous dancing, singing, fasting, and activities that to outsiders appear impossibly long and hard. The truth is that they are not so difficult once you accept participating fully in the present moment.

Exercise: Take ten minutes out and wander aimlessly about. You may wish to go outside or stay indoors but make sure that in this ten minutes you accomplish absolutely nothing. No TV, no radio, no newspaper, no music, no thinking, no making lists, no planning, no recalling, no figuring out, no eating, no going to the bathroom, no trimming your nails, no smoking or drinking, no sexual fantasies, no anything. Just be wandering around looking at things and experiencing being alive.

Prayer to Help Erase Impatience

*C*reator

You have forever

You are in no hurry

You are the one who created time

You have all the time you want

And you can end time whenever you want to

And you would still be you

You are outside of time

And you are in time

Always in perfect time

But I somehow got the idea that I am time limited

I became afraid I would run out of time

I made time my god and my master

I made time more important than anything else

Creator, you dreamed me up to be like you

To be outside of time

You gave me time to use as a tool

So that I can enjoy the physical world

And savor it

I have time

All the time I need to accomplish what I
came for

I am in time, in the rhythm of my life

I am in the rhythm of the cycles and beats of
nature

The more I slow my mind down, the more I
get done

The more I slow myself down, the more
connected *I am*

I have time

Time is mine to use

I am the master of time and time is my
servant

I have time to think

I have time to feel

I have time to act

I have time to be

I have time to become

I have time for others

And I have time for myself

I am in time, in the rhythm of my life

I am beyond time

I have all time

I create time and stretch it out as I need it

I collapse time when *I am* enjoying what I
am doing

I play with time because time is flexible
Time is an illusion because *I am* beyond time
I am in time, in the rhythm of my life

STUBBORNNESS

When we are afraid of change, because our experience of it has been painful, we do everything in our power to put the brakes on. We pull back into a corner of safety and refuse to budge, rejecting all other points of view. We stop listening to anything that is not in accordance with our own point of view. Sometimes our stubbornness causes us to become rebellious against new directives or orders because we do not like to be told what to do. This comes from long experience of being ordered around and forced to comply as children. We hate it when choice is taken away from us because freedom is so valuable that we have exaggerated reactions to the perception that it is being taken away. We react with stubbornness and that stance is harmful to relationships and to our own happiness.

Shaman teachers do everything in their power to break their apprentices of stubbornness because they know that it can become an insurmountable block to power and freedom. Stubbornness can have no place on the shamanic path to freedom and infinity.

The first order of business then is to relax the tension of 'holding against' in order to become more flexible. Here are four suggestions for initially dealing with stubbornness.

EXERCISES:

1. Get a massage where you particularly focus on having your back loosened up. Likewise have the practitioner work with your jaw and pelvis.

2. Say yes more often and see what happens.

3. Initiate change yourself as often as possible.

4. Practice truly listening to others points of view especially when they differ from your own.

Prayer for Dealing with Stubbornness

Creator, you create all change
Yet I was afraid of change
I thought I could stop change from
    happening
By saying no and refusing to listen
I thought that if I didn't listen I would be
    safe
Like the child who covers their ears and
    hums
When they don't like what they hear
I thought that by tightening up my back
And holding my jaw tight shut
I could keep my world safe like a closed nut
I got angry when I was forced to comply
I got angry when I was given no choice

I tried to preserve my integrity

By rebelling and doing the opposite

But this wasn't free either

I was caught in a trap

But change seems to happen anyway

Because the world is not fixed in any way or
form

You create the world anew millions of times a
second

And who can try to stop that

You are like a freight train

Coming fast down the tracks at full speed

And I am free to hop aboard

Or I can stand in the tracks and hold up my
hands

And the train is not going to stop or stand

Creator you made me to evolve

You made me to adapt and readapt

And leave behind all form

This world only seems fixed at times

But is actually flowing like a great river

I am like you and I am changing by the
second

All the particles in my body are rearranging
constantly

I never step into the same world from
moment to moment

Because you are renewing it effortlessly
I am an evolving creature
Changing and adapting
And when I relax I grow
I am like you in every way
And I am made to be free
So to you I say yes
To you I listen
To you I do what you tell me
And you are in everyone everywhere
So what is there to resist
You made me free
You made me to change
And when I do I meet you in all your
     stupendous glory

LOW SELF-ESTEEM

In a world of fierce competition as we live in there are few
winners and many losers, just like in a lottery game. There are
a few superstars whom we worship as a society and then there
is everyone else. With so much potential for rejection,
judgment, and abandonment it is quite difficult at times to
maintain a healthy self-esteem. If we are strong and have been
supported well in our early years we gain confidence to face

these challenges. But if we have been criticized endlessly, put down, compared, judged, found wanting, or have been ignored our self-esteem suffers and the slightest criticism can be very hard to accept.

If we struggle with low self-esteem then we tend to apologize for ourselves too much. We often don't try things because we feel we will utterly fail and we accept lower standards or demand less of life because we don't feel worthy. This is a scourge that limits our enjoyment of life and unfortunately gets passed on to our children and all the following generations like a disease. Fortunately there is a cure for low self-esteem. Shamans would say that feeling inferior is a result of not truly understanding the true nature of reality and not understanding whom 'we are' spiritually speaking. Reconnecting with Spirit is the ultimate answer.

Prayer to Enhance Self-Esteem

Great Spirit

I forgot for a while that you made me

I thought that I was poor quality
    merchandise

I even came to believe that I was less than
    others

I thought I was dumb and clumsy

I thought I was unattractive, perhaps too
    thin or too fat

I thought I was socially inept and had
    nothing to say

I thought nobody could possibly want me

I didn't love myself

Thought my body was off

I believed my nose wasn't right

My hair was bad, my skin was rough

I was just a mess

I was always last chosen

I believed I was not cool

I thought I had to settle for less

I believed I had no voice to stand up for
myself

So I accepted abuse

I thought I was a big accident

I forgot for a while that you made me

And all that actually meant

Why did you create me? Did you really make
such a worm?

Of course I am mistaken

What an insult to you to criticize your creation

You made me out of yourself

You are creating me now from your own
dreaming

That is a total honor and gift

But did I fail you? Am I turning gold into
lead?

No, how can that be, I cannot override your
creation

You are making me now, moment by moment

How can that be a failure

You made me out of yourself

With an enormous outpouring of love

I share in your beauty

I share in your intelligence

I share in your expansiveness

I breathe you in, I breathe you out

You are inside of me now

I look at my arms, I look at my hands

These are yours that *I am* seeing

I see my reflection and *I am* seeing you

What a mistake to disparage what you are
   making

I'm sorry for insulting you, for putting you
   down

I am your perfect child

I am you

You are me and without you I become
   diminished

Yet with you *I am* filled with light

I shine with vitality

I am wonderful

I am potential

I am becoming

I am capable

I am fulfilling your plan

I am being

And how can being be wrong when what *I am* being is you

ON FEARING INTIMACY

At the deepest levels of our being, we all want to be connected, loved, and nurtured. At the spiritual level this is a fact but on a body level the fact feels like a lie. Many of us spend a lifetime looking for that one special person who is our soulmate, who will make everything feel right and complete. Too often we never find that fantasy person but instead we find real live people, flawed, defensive, insecure, and fearful. We are afraid of these people because they are too much like us and since we don't accept ourselves, we don't want to accept them. We avoid getting close because we might want too much from them, might be too dependent, might show our own vulnerabilities and flaws, and fear abandonment by these very people we judge to be flawed. What a dilemma! The only solution is to love whomever is here on Earth with us, to let down our guard, take the risk, and be vulnerable while at the same time exercising good judgment. How do we discriminate and at the same time be available? That is not so difficult as it seems. Our job is to be available. Spirit's job is to help us discriminate.

Prayer for Intimacy and Relationship

For a long time I walked alone
Feeling isolated, wishing, and hoping for
Someone to love
Someone to love me

But when someone came near
I put up walls, I ran away out of fear
I just couldn't take the risk
To let myself get close

So, I picked those I always knew
Would never get close to me
That's a game I played
But I lied and told myself I just wasn't lucky

Spirit I'll tell you the truth
I want to be close
I've just been afraid
I am no longer interested in isolation

I am willing to let you in
I am not alone anyway, never have been
You have always been with me
You will always be with me

And I know I meet you in everyone
But not all people are right for me
Some of them are afraid to get close too
And they are not good for me to be with

Spirit, you send me someone I can trust
You discriminate and decide who is best
I charge you each day to direct me
To know who to seek

I trust you to send me who I need
I will keep my heart open
Send me a partner to love and respect
One who wants to share

Someone who is patient with me
Someone who wants to meet Spirit in me
I am finding connection through you
I am discovering deep partnership

And meanwhile I will be a friend
To all beings who express you freely
And I will meet you in everyone
And I will be present for you and give you
    warmth

I am privileged to be your friend
You who give me and all things life
That is where relationship starts
That is where intimacy begins

DEALING WITH ENEMIES

No matter how nice people say you are, it is almost inevitable that you are going to have an enemy at some time and some place. Shamans are exceptionally aware of this fact and develop numerous techniques to deal with it because for them it can be a life or death proposition. As long as there is jealousy, misunderstanding, envy, competition, and fear, enemies will be a part of this world. Enemies can make your life miserable yet they can teach you many valuable things about yourself. I have had my share of enemies in my life: one who took a woman away from me; one who ruined a book project; another who stole vast sums of money from me; and one who succeeded in eliminating a teaching job I truly loved because she disagreed with my philosophy. My enemies have taught me more than I could ever have imagined. Mostly they showed me where my fears lay, where my insecurities were, and where I needed clearer boundaries.

A Prayer to Handle Enmity

*G*reat Spirit

I cannot always control how people feel
    about me
I cannot always prevent them from trying to
    do me harm
What I can do is practice seeing the seeds of
    Spirit in them
With attention and focus I can see their
    humanity and their divinity

I can see their hurt, their fear
I can understand my own fear and choose to
    go beyond it
I may have to stop them from harming me
I may have to prevent actions they take

Yet in meditation I will offer them flowers
I will give them an olive branch
I will send them love and respect
And whatever they truly desire behind their
    enmity

What fires their heart is what fires mine
What charges their aliveness charges mine
We have the same source

We have the same destination

And while we play out our chess moves
    outwardly
Inwardly they are my brothers, they are my
    sisters
They are my future friends
Ones who I will one day cherish

Someone who I will learn to love
One who perhaps one day will save my life
Or rescue me from prison
Or will give me a home

Everything comes around
And if I hold no ill will toward them
Hatred will die on the vine
And love will gradually find a hold

Part Nine:

Praying for Others and for Conditions

Shamanically speaking, praying for others is more complex than praying for yourself for a number of reasons. You should first learn to pray for yourself effectively and then when you begin getting results and have a track record, you are ready to pray for others. Here are some of the reasons why:

- Firstly you don't always know what is best for another even if your intentions are good. Perhaps their own essence that is directly connected with Spirit knows that an illness will teach them something they can learn no other way. Perhaps it is their time to die and no matter how much you pray you will not be able to save them.

- Secondly the person you pray for has to desire to be healed or helped in some way or they will not be able to benefit from your prayers. Sometimes they have a hidden agenda around their illness or problem and they might be unwilling to give it up. Maybe they desire to punish someone else by being sick or they want people to feel sorry for them.

Perhaps they feel so unworthy of help that they cannot conceive of receiving assistance and they block any path that would lead them out of their difficulty. There are many reasons a person might not want to be helped or may not allow help in.

- Thirdly if you do not pray correctly for someone you may actually be doing her or him more harm than good. If you regard them as weak and ineffective, so much so that you believe without your help they will surely go under, then you are pouring energy into skepticism about them and this will only increase their problem.

Therefore be careful when you pray for others and yet realize that there are also excellent reasons to pray for them as well. Praying for another is a way of loving them and almost everyone is in great need of more love. Sometimes someone is in such a bad way that they are unable to pray for themselves and your prayers can be powerfully effective in helping them out of a bad spot. If they are under anesthesia, are unconscious, terribly anxious, seriously depressed, or are in terrific pain they may strongly need your prayers. If your prayers for another are genuine and coming from a loving state, then your prayers are never wasted. Even if they cannot receive the content of your prayers at this time, your love does reach them and this helps no matter what, even if they die. By praying for them you may make their death easier than it might have been without your intercession. Here are some guidelines to help you pray for another in a powerful and effective way.

1. Always ask permission from Spirit before you start

praying for someone. Become quiet and go to the *I Am* place. Then ask if your prayers are for that person's greatest good at this time. If you have trouble receiving a clear answer, an effective technique is to see if you get a red light or a green light in response to your question. If green, pray away. If red do not overrule it. Let them be.

2. If you receive permission to go ahead, then ask Spirit to support your prayers and to provide the person for whom you are praying with what they need the most at this time. Sometimes you are shown exactly what to pray for, sometimes not.

3. Go back to the *I Am* place and reconnect with your own essence. You might wish to follow the following format:

Prayer for Healing Another Person

Spirit, *I am* praying for ....
I am asking that he/ she be healed of
....
(Let's say the condition is migraine
   headaches)
Migraines, be gone from ....

(visualize darkness leaving from their head and dissipating in a violet flame. You may move your hands in a gesture to disperse the darkness and cast it into a candle flame or the like)

Migraines, leave .... now

Migraines, you have no power over
....

Spirit, allow ....at this time to learn
whatever the migraines have been trying to
teach him/her.

Allow him/her to receive this information at
the deepest levels of his/her awareness so
this condition no longer prevails.

At this time *I am* intending that
................receive special assistance to
heal him/her from migraines.

Send the most powerful inner healing
specialist to work with him/her on healing
the condition.

May he/she never experience this condition
again.

Migraines are now gone

His/her head feels bright and clear

(visualize the person smiling brightly and headache-free.
Flood their head with bright metallic gold that is radiating a
turquoise or green light)

You may be successful the first time you pray. If the person's
ailment persists do not allow this to discourage you. Persist
with your shamanic praying and decreeing in this fashion and

they will be benefited in the long run.

SEEKING PROTECTION FOR OTHERS

These days with the uncertainty of terrorism, war, and spreading disease you may be concerned about loved ones traveling afar or living in areas of the world that have become dangerous. Certainly you cannot physically protect everyone you love or care for but you can always turn to the power of prayer to assist them from within. Many young men and women have been protected in horrific war zones and dangerous duty because someone far away sought for and sent protection to them. Many Native American soldiers returned unscathed from horrific battle during World War II and Vietnam because they had shamans and family members praying and doing ceremony for them from afar.

If you are seeking protection for a loved one who may be in harm's way you may wish to pray the following way. Notice that the prayer actually directs Spirit toward what you want to accomplish.

Prayer for Protection of Another

Spirit, *I am* praying for ....
I am asking that he/she be surrounded by
    your powerful protection
Surround............... with your brilliant
    blue protective light

(visualize this bright blue cover of protective light surrounding them from head to foot)

> May he/she be always protected
> May he/she walk through danger unscathed
> May................ be safe to complete all
> his/her goals and make all his/her
> wonderful contributions
> May harmful actions and thoughts pass
> him/her by
> Let............ walk in light and safety

(visualize them walking safely through all matter of challenges. Everything bounces off the protective blue light that surrounds them. Repeat this three times)

PRAYING FOR PEACE AND BIG PROBLEMS IN THE WORLD

Sometimes you may wish to pray for a much bigger scenario such as peace in the world, the reduction of hostilities between two countries, or that suffering be lifted and that thousands of people receive food and health care. There is almost no limit to the number of world situations that you can pray for at this time. You may feel that you are too inconsequential to have an impact on such a large situation or a world problem that is geographically distant but you would be wrong to think so. Sincere prayers with strong intent coming from just one individual can have an amazing impact on the whole. Chances are others are praying for help as well and their prayers will join yours for a larger impact because shamanically speaking like attracts like.

Here is a suggestion regarding how to pray effectively for the bigger picture.

Prayer for Peace

*S*pirit, *I am* praying for ....(or)
  I am praying for world peace.

(go to the *I am* place and say '*I am* light' several times.)

  I am light
  I am light
  I am light

(Allow this light to burn brightly like a golden sun in your chest. Allow the sun in your chest to expand and glowingly fill your entire chest and then let it set the rest of your body on fire so that your entire body is glowing like a bright sun.)

  Spirit, may there be peace in this world.
  I am peaceful
  I am peace

(Now allow the golden light to expand out into the space all around you

Allow this light to spread outside your immediate vicinity to all the countryside and all the communities nearby.)

I am light
I am light
I am light

I am peace
I am peace
I am peace

(Now continue to see the golden light spreading from your chest out into the world, crossing mountains and oceans and spreading like a wave around the globe. Allow this golden light to become many colors of the rainbow, bathing the areas that have special needs so that they may absorb the exact colors that they require at this time.)

I am light
I am light
I am light

I am peace
I am peace
I am peace

I am love
I am love
I am love

You may continue in this fashion for as long as you like. Then gradually mentally return to where you are sitting. Gandhi said that if you want something to become reality then you must become it first. If you want peace in the world then you must become it. He was more than right. That is why this prayer is set up the way that it is. While it may sound odd, in fact it is designed to produce the maximum beneficial effect. It becomes even more powerful when said in a group and everyone participates in the vision of light spreading to wherever it is needed most.

PRAYING TO CHANGE A CONDITION

Sometimes there is a condition in your environment that you would like to change or ameliorate such as drought, intense heat or cold, or dangerous tornadoes, hurricanes, and wind storms. While usually nature knows what it is doing and does not need any help, there are times when a little prayer can shift a storm just enough to offer protection for you and your loved ones. The great master shamans all knew how to address the weather and it would bend to their will if they asked it to. They knew that nature is in the domain of Spirit so that commanding the weather is like talking to God directly. Therefore in order to obtain a change of condition you must address the weather itself. You are much more likely to get results if you express gratitude and show respect. Here is an example of how.

A Prayer for Rain

Spirit, you are in these coming Clouds
You are so beautiful and magnificent
You have come to us so many times before
And given us your precious water
Thank you for your generosity and kindness
Thank you for making the land green and
    rich
Thank you for filling the rivers and lakes
Thank you for providing us with water to
    drink
Spirit in the Clouds, gather together once
    again strong and moist
Use your light to gather the beautiful drops
    of moisture
Send the rain that we are so in need of
Pour your rich liquid onto this land
That our brothers and sisters, the plants and
    animals may drink deeply
That they may be happy and full
That we may benefit from your bounty as
    well
Fill our streams and reservoirs once again
Feel our love magnetizing you this way

Feel our wish for rain and come this way

And we will not forget your generosity

And we will not forget your kindness

You are so giving

We are so fortunate

Come this way

Come this way

Come this way

Strongly visualize the clouds gathering and rain coming to the land. See drops of water congealing around tiny points of brilliant light. Feel gladness in your heart as you see, sense, and feel the fresh rain gathering into clouds and falling upon the landscape. Smell the new rain as it moisturizes the air and the soil making everything damp and steamy.

WHEN THERE IS TOO MUCH OF SOMETHING

Sometimes the land receives too much rain and the result is flooding, loss of life and property damage. While fire is good for the land, too much can be terribly destructive and the same can be true for wind, cold, and heat. To pray for relief is not so different from praying for more. One should approach Spirit with respect and gratitude first, then state what is needed. While it may sound strange to you to address the elements directly, this is the way it has always been done by shamans around the world. They know that the elements respond to human commands if done properly. That is why the Bible states that man was given dominion over the Earth, not to destroy it or plunder it, but to work with it cooperatively.

A Prayer for Protection from Fire

*G*reat Spirit

You have given us a wonderful tool by giving
us fire

Fire warms us and is good for the land

You gave us the fire of the sun that radiates
to us the conditions for life

You gave us the fire of our emotions to create
with

You gave us the fire of metabolism to digest
our food

You gave us the fire of the life force within
each atom of our bodies

You gave us the fire of electricity to light our
way

To run our tools and live a better life

Spirit, thank you for this great gift you have
given us for free

Help us to always use the power of fire well
and productively

Protect us from too much heat and fire that
is out of control

May fire be contained to do good yet keep us
from harm

Sacred fire, lower your flames that we may
live

Powerful fire, move to where you are most
needed

Fire contain your smoke and heat and stop
advancing here

Fire, you answer to Spirit and I have asked
Spirit to contain you

You are my friend and I cannot exist without
you

Hear my prayer now

Part Ten:

Advanced Shamanic Techniques of Prayer

"*I am* you, you are me, come together, right now'
(Beatles)

Working with 'I Am'

We discussed the importance of the words 'I Am' at the beginning of this book. Now here is a chance to work with 'I Am' as a power tool. Remember that there is no other phrase quite as powerful for creating as the 'I Am' phrase because it is in alignment with the Creator. Your 'I Am' is your essence. When you say these words you invoke your own essence self, your greater self that goes way beyond your ego or false self. In spiritual literature this 'I Am' presence has often been referred to as Lord or Father. Shamans refer to it as Spirit, The Central Sun, Great Provider, and many other names. You can call it whatever you wish as long as you realize that it is the part of you that is related directly to the Creator.

Here are several ways to work with 'I Am'. Do not approach this lightly because the work is sacred, powerful, and needs to be approached respectfully.

'I Am' Practice One: 'I am Light; I am the Sun'

Find a quiet place to be where you will not be interrupted for a while. Lying down or sitting is excellent. After you become acquainted with this exercise you may wish to close your eyes except for a little slit. Begin by breathing deeply into your lungs. Place your attention on your chest and specifically in the center of your heart. Imagine that in the center of your heart is a single atom that is the spark that generates your whole being. That atom is being given to you by the Creator at this very moment for you to be conscious and alive. Shamanically speaking it is a tiny replica of the sun in the sky and is connected with it energetically. Realize the communication this atom has with the powerful radiant sun in the sky. They are one.

As you breathe into the core of this atom and as you breathe out begin to say out loud, '*I Am*'. You may choose to say the words only on the out breathe or 'I' on the in breath and 'Am' on the out breath. Go slowly and savor each time you say it. Try placing the emphasis on each word differently and sense what happens.

After a time begin to say '*I Am* light' and get a sense of a brilliant light generating from the single atom. So bright is the light that it expands out in blinding brilliance from your chest and sends rays out to every part of your body. You may experience the radiation of this light expanding in every direction just like the sun, all through the community, the country, the world, possibly out into the universe. On its way it envelops all world leaders and enters their hearts reminding them of the great loving light of Source.

Now expand your statement to say '*I Am* the light of the Sun.' Become a living, radiant, glowing Sun and continue your radiation to the places of greatest need.

Stay with the sense of being created each second. Be aware that your being awake and aware is a fabulous blessing. Thank spirit for making you if you wish. Continue with '*I am* the light of the Sun.' Be aware of the profound miracle of being alive. Stay with the glad to be alive point in the middle of your heart. Be aware of how good this feels. If you wish press on your sternum where you feel good. Stay with this as long as you like. Do it often and miracles will definitely happen.

'I AM' PRACTICE TWO: BEING THAT

Now, if you wish, begin to look around the room or the environment you are in. As your eyes fix on something expand the phrase '*I Am*' to '*I Am that*'. Be aware that you are whatever you are looking at. Begin to get the sense that you are creating that thing in your experience and that it is not separate from you. When you breathe in go back to your chest. When you breathe out go out to objects around you, '*I Am that.*' '*I Am that.*' '*I Am that.*' If you wish you may take a walk and continue the process of '*I Am that.*' This is also something you can do on a long trip in the car. Be sure to include the sun, the moon, the stars, the clouds, the ocean, the mountains, and great forests and deserts. Expect to become very high.

You may also return to this prayer briefly before an important presentation, meeting, or phone call. '*I Am*' makes you fully present very quickly and it makes you powerful.

ON WAKING UP

Waking up shamanically and spiritually speaking has to do with a great many variables including your actual readiness, your maturity, your experience, your desire for it, your feelings of worthiness, and a host of other influences. If you have read this far in this book you are probably quite ready and have already wakened to some degree. There are ways to become more fully awake. One profound way is to become aware of the area where your spine enters your skull at the base of the brain. There is a structure there called the medulla oblongata. You might wish to consult an anatomy book and take a look at it. It is like a little snake with a flower on the end. In spiritual literature the flower has been referred to as the 'mouth of God'. Paramahansa Yogananda and many other great spiritual teachers have spoken about the significance and importance of this structure to consciousness.

Spirit or your essence connects to your body in two primary places. One is through the top of the head down into the center of your heart. The other is through the top of the head and into the medulla where it divides and distributes itself through tiny filaments into every atom of the body, keeping you alive and conscious. If these connections are withdrawn, your body dies immediately.

The following is a powerful concentration that was recommended in part by Paramahansa Yogananda. Remember that you are working with very powerful forces here. If you are not ready, nothing will happen. If you are ready you will experience an expansion of your awareness and consciousness.

'I Am' Practice Three: Waking Up

Sit quietly in an undisturbed place.

Breathe regularly into your chest and focus on your heart.

As you breathe out say '*I Am*' several times.

Now switch your attention and focus on the base of your brain.

Envision a brilliant golden light there and as you breathe out, say '*I Am*'. If you find it helpful you can imagine the words printed on the base of your brain at the location of the medulla.

Keep your eyes focused upward to the point between your eyebrows.

From the little flower at the top of the medulla imagine rays of brilliant golden light streaming upward toward your eyes.

Allow the rays to stream out of your eyes.

Now imagine a third ray streaming out of the point between your eyebrows.

There is now a little triad of rays of golden light streaming out of your medulla out of your eyes and where tradition says your third eye is.

Allow a portion of this light to bounce back to the medulla again so that a circulation of golden light begins.

Continue for as long as you wish.

Conclusion

Now you have been exposed to the spiritual technology of shamanic prayer. Nothing you have read in this book is new. All the information is as old as the proverbial hills but here it has been presented in a way that perhaps is new and accessible for you. The prayers found their way into my life and now they have been passed on to you. As a result maybe you will be able to build your own spontaneous prayers that vastly transform your experience of Spirit within your life.

Without prayer our lives are often a great struggle, lacking in direction or support. With prayer the dynamic changes radically to one of evolving participation and quantum leaps of awakening. Praying is quite literally talking to Spirit in such a way as to get into the main current of our life-stream, a quickening, heart opening, powerful development that makes life a dance in the garden rather than a crawl through the briars.

The great shamans and saints have all said that their prayers led them deeper into a life of constantly talking to Spirit and ever listening for the great wisdom that emerged from their after-prayer silence. May you also be showered with such blessings and exalted graces.

About the Authors

José and his wife Lena have completed a ten-year apprentice-ship with a high degree Huichol shaman living in the Sierras of Mexico and have specific training with Shipibo shamans in the Amazon and with Pacos in the Andes regions of Peru. In addition they have studied with and visited with shamans in central Australia, Nepal, Finland, Kenya and the American South-west. José is a Doctor of Psychology.

Power Path Seminars™, José Stevens, coaching and consulting business uses the principles outlined in his books. With Power Path Seminars ™ he brings over thirty years of experience to his many clients through effective guidance programs, retreats, trainings, and seminars. In addition PPS provides accreditation and certification for consultants and coaches.

José and Lena are the authors of *Secrets of Shamanism: Tapping the Spirit Power Within You,* (Avon, 1988). In addition to numerous other books and articles, Dr Jose Stevens is the author of *The Power Path: The Shaman's Way to Success in Business and Life,* (New World Library, 2002) and *Transforming Your Dragons: Turning Fear Patterns into Personal Power,* released in 1994 by Bear and Company.

Dr José Stevens has his base of operations in Santa Fe, New Mexico, and lectures internationally, teaching about principles of power, prosperity, personality types, communi-cation styles, peak performance, and self-development. José has consulted with various individuals and businesses in Japan, Canada, Venezuela, Iceland, England, Finland, and Russia and both Lena and José have led many tour groups to the ancient sacred sites of Egypt, England, the Yucatan, and Peru.

In addition, José provides consultation with lawyers, business leaders, scientists and entrepreneurs from coast to coast and includes Hollywood producers, actors and screenwriters among his high profile clients. He uses his knowledge of shamanism and business psychology to privately coach and assist leaders to make difficult life decisions and to develop business strategy. His diverse client group regularly reports powerful results.

Available Products and Services through Power Path Seminars

Monthly newsletter offering cultural trends and current events articles
Tapes on a variety of topics including Mediation and Prayer
Individual and group coaching and consultation
Training seminars
Certification programs
Wilderness retreats, solos, and quests
Continuing education

Check the website for a current schedule of classes, workshops, lectures, retreats, and other events:

Website: powerpathseminars.com
E-mail the author at: *Pivotal@pivres.com*
Power Path Seminars
P.O. Box 272
Santa Fe, New Mexico 87504-0272
Phone: (505) 982-8732